RIVER RUNNERS' RECIPES

BY PATRICIA McCAIREN

Menasha Ridge Press

To ravenous river runners everywhere.

Copyright © 1991, 1994 by Patricia McCairen
Printed in the United States of America

Library of Congress Cataloging-in-Publication Data

McCairen, Patricia, 1940-
    River runners' recipies/by Patricia McCairen.
        p. cm.

Includes index.
ISBN 0-89732-109-X
1. Outdoor cookery.   I. Title.
TX823.M35   1991   641.5 '78   91-14725 CIP

Design by Judy Petry
Illustrations by Constance Bollen
Cover design and illustration by Leslie Cummins

Menasha Ridge Press
3169 Cahaba Heights Road
Birmingham, AL 35243

CONTENTS

ACKNOWLEDGMENTS

I would like to extend special thanks to John Cassidy for the time he spent editing this manuscript at various stages and for the knowledge I gained from his expertise. Thanks also to Erin Wilson, who put so much time and effort into the beginning stages of the book and gave me the support I needed. And, finally, thanks to the following people for their time, support, and suggestions, all of which made this book possible: Gail Burton, Pat Davis, Sparky Kramer, Carol Nelson, David Noyes, Tim Palmer, Bette Savitt, Patricia Schifferle, and Steve Tichenor.

PRELIMINARIES

As soon as the first sign of spring appears, I find myself thinking almost constantly of rivers. Their beauty, tranquillity, and wildness come to mind, and the thought of seeing new rivers and running old favorites draws me like a magnet back to their rippling waters. Nothing sings to me quite like a river; nothing is so thrilling as running a challenging rapid.

With those first days of spring, I begin taking equipment out of winter storage, checking it over, and making plans for future trips. The pace picks up as time for the trip draws nearer. Gear must be assembled, people gathered, a shuttle arranged, and food purchased. Sometimes the latter is put off until the last minute, and the menu is haphazard and disappointing. Whether your needs dictate a simple piece of fruit and a drink or an elaborate gourmet repast, careful meal planning will enhance everyone's enjoyment of a trip. I hope to provide ideas and suggestions that will assist all those who wish to dine well while floating their favorite river.

River trips offer a luxurious approach to wilderness camping. Weight, up to a point, is not a major consideration. A rubber raft, drift boat, dory, or canoe can carry those culinary items that make dining so delightful. Once you master the simple arts of packing, storing, and cooking outdoors, you can make gourmet meals a part of your river trip.

The recipes that follow emphasize nutrition, variety, and simplicity. They are suitable for any river trip, whether it be long or short, in hot climes or cold. Most are one-pot meals—the fewer the dishes the better. While specific quantities are given for each ingredient, many of the recipes lend themselves to creative cookery. Many were invented on one of the numerous rivers in this country: hence the names, taken from those wonderful rivers, side canyons, and beaches that endear themselves to those of us who relish floating down a torrent of moving water.

Menu Planning

The river has beckoned and you've set a time for your trip. Now it is a simple matter of getting your friends together, acquiring the necessary equipment, and planning the menu. (It sounds so easy, doesn't it?!)

Your inclination may be to plan the menu alone. Don't do it. Though you be Julia Child herself, your friends might not like your selection of meals. Discovering this at the bottom of a river canyon can be a painful experience. I once made the mistake of planning a thirty-two-day menu for eleven people by myself. Once on the river, I was never free of the kitchen, and complaints came regularly from the other trip members. If, despite your best efforts to do otherwise, you are still left planning the menu alone, at least have the others go over it and make comments. Without this precaution, you may wish you were doing a solo trip.

Judging food quantity is often the most difficult part of menu planning. A canoeing trip with a number of portages will increase appetites, as will cold, rainy weather or rivers with demanding rapids that bring on a high adrenalin rush. As hungry boaters are more prone to accidents, it is important to keep energy levels up. Carbohydrates are an excellent source of energy for boaters using calories at a faster rate than usual. It is best to avoid refined sugar, however, as it only provides a brief burst of energy before dropping you lower than you were before eating it. Plan high protein meals whenever long, hard days are anticipated. If meat does not appeal to you, use one of the many protein combination dishes among the recipes (dairy and wheat, beans and rice, beans and cheese, dairy and potatoes, for example).

On long trips, give some thought to the order of meals. Perishable foods should be eaten first, obviously, while durable items can be served later in the trip. If weight is a problem because your canoeing route requires a number of portages or your fourteen-foot raft is the only support for ten kayakers, you may wish to take fewer canned goods. You can eliminate some weight by planning your menu to include more dry goods and produce.

Weather is another factor you should take into account when planning a menu. In the spring, when cold, rainy days may prevail, choose meals that are simple to prepare and that will stick to the ribs. Forget about making a quiche and go for one-pot meals like Noodle-Cheese-Nut Thing, Briggs's Beans, and Hermit Creek Potato Soup that heat up in a short time. For hot weather trips, try serving cold dishes like Dr. Rouzer's Gazpacho, Dolores River Tabouleh, and other salads which may be more refreshing than a heavier dish. Even in hot weather salt may be eliminated as a seasoning, as most foods already contain ample amounts of sodium.

A certain amount of organization will definitely help in planning a workable menu. I've used three basic menu styles successfully and like each. Once you've selected a menu plan, write it down and store it in the staples box where it is readily available. Following are examples of each menu plan along with comments on their individual merits.

The first, and no doubt most logical, entails planning the menu for each day of the trip, beginning and ending with lunch.

Day 1   **Lunch:**   Stanislaus Guacamole
Tortillas
Juice
Peanut butter and jam
Cookies

Dinner:	Basic Brown Rice
	Tamari Chicken
	Sprouts Salad
	Peshtigo Cheesecake

Day 2   **Breakfast:**   Orange juice
Morning Crank
Allagash French Toast
Syrup

	Lunch:	Red Wall Cavern Spread
		Crackers
		Juice
		Peanut butter and jam
		Dates and figs

. . . and so on, for any length trip.

As you can see, a daily menu is tightly structured so nothing is left to chance. It is easy to draw up and is the most reliable and easiest plan to use. Even inexperienced river runners can look up the recipe and make the meal. Daily planning reduces the risk of overbuying and of food spoilage. I would advise using a daily menu whenever order is necessary to facilitate a guide's work or with inexperienced groups.

A second menu plan allows more flexibility. Recipes are selected for a trip and arranged by meal rather than by day. On long trips, certain meals may be made more than once. To keep track of meals that have been eaten (it is easier to forget than you might think), place a small box next to each selection. After making a recipe, check off the box. A bill of fare midway through a five-day trip might look like this:

Breakfasts: ☑ Rio Grande Huevos Rancheros
☐ American River Scromlet
☑ Early Morning Mix
☐ Arkansas River Apple Cakes
☐ Riverbank Muffins

Lunches: ☑ Harper's Bizarre
☑ Little Colorado Hummus
☐ Marjene's Cheese Spread
☐ Youghiogheny Egg Salad
☑ Hiwassee River Combo

Salads: ☐ Gauley Bean Salad
☑ Ferg's Zephyr Salad
☑ Selway Greek Salad

Dinners: ☐ Eel River Tostados
☑ Cataract Canyon Lasagna
☑ Hells Canyon Stroganoff
☐ Potato Cheese Bake

Desserts: ☑ Variety Sweet Loaf
☐ Boundary Waters Apple Crisp
☐ Androscoggin Dessert

I've used this plan often, usually on trips longer than two weeks, or with a small, very experienced group. I like the freedon it allows the *chef de cuisine* to make up her or his own menu. But the flexibility of an open menu can create problems. It may not be enough structure for someone hesitant about outdoor or group cooking. The actual planning takes more care, since meals can be forgotten and important ingredients left off the shopping list. But if you enjoy being on a flexible schedule and prefer to choose your meals to fit the day's activities, this is a good menu to use.

The third plan is truly a group endeavor. Each person on the trip is totally responsible for the planning and preparing of a particular meal (or meals). Your written menu plan would look like this:

	Breakfasts	**Lunches**	**Dinners**
Day 1		Gail	Russell
Day 2	Ronit	Tom	Marian
Day 3	Dwight	Melinda	

...and so on.

I first used this method on a five-day Rogue River trip with a group of ten independent, experienced people. At breakfast, the day before put-in, we divided up the meals—one person on each of the four dinners and four breakfasts and two people making the five lunches. An element of surprise was added when everyone decided to keep his or her menus a secret. Right after breakfast we hit the grocery store en masse, finished the shopping quickly, and headed to put-in. Not only was this fun, but each one of us seemed challenged to come up with creative meals. Did we eat well!

Each of the menu plans can be used in conjunction with this book by writing down the name of the recipe and perhaps the page number. This will help the inexperienced, and no one can use the excuse: "I can't cook." If they can read they can cook!

If you don't wish to take this book on the river, make menu cards. Each card can contain three meals, beginning with dinner and ending with lunch. When using cards, remember to include all the ingredients used in each meal and possibly some simple instructions.

With each plan it is necessary to stick to the menu, because provisions have been purchased accordingly. Dipping impulsively into the food stores might necessitate some unusual concoctions late in the trip.

After planning a menu, make out a shopping list. Go over each meal carefully and note all ingredients so nothing will be forgotten.

You will also need items that do not appear on a food list or in menus. These include:

Garbage bags. A variety of sizes and weights are available. Four-gallon bags are good for trips of up to ten people. Use one for each dinner, breakfast, and lunch. Thirty-gallon bags come in different weights and are useful for larger groups. One bag may do for all three meals. Once full, small bags are easier to store than larger ones, but smaller bags are thinner and break more easily. Heavy duty garbage bags can also be used as liners in stuff sacks to keep personal effects handy and dry. Pack extra garbage bags on every trip.

Freezer and Ziploc bags. These bags are handy for storing leftover food, carrying cake or pancake mixes, holding damaged boxes in order to keep the staples box clean, keeping matches dry, protecting this book or menu cards from food and water, and many other uses that come up regularly while on the river. Keep extras in the staples box for emergencies.

Matches. You can't do without them. Buy the large, wooden, strike-anywhere type, three boxes to a package. Store in waterproof containers. Place one in staples, one in commissary, and another in a private stash.

Dish soap. A twelve-ounce bottle should be enough for a week-long trip.

Hand soap. Have a five-ounce bar at the kitchen hand-wash and another at the porta-potty. They will last at least a couple of weeks.

Clorox. A quart is enough for an eight-day trip, used both morning and evening in the dishpails.

Scrubber. One scrubber will last a couple of trips—unless you burn pots a lot.

Sponges. Buy a few—there is a sponge stealing monster on every river. Sponges also commit suicide and collect grunge with great regularity.

Paper towels. One roll per week, but use sparingly.

Charcoal briquets. Bags of five, ten, and twenty pounds are available. A ten-pound bag should bake about six ten-inch Dutch ovens or eight eight-inch Dutch ovens.

Lighter fluid. Commonly known as Boy Scout juice. Lighter fluid is useful for starting fires, especially if wood is damp or slightly green. Also, lighter fluid is essential to start charcoal briquets if you don't have a camp-fire.

Coleman or propane fuel. Each stove uses fuel at a different rate. Become familiar with your stove and take plenty of fuel, especially when it is not possible to have a campfire.

Aluminum foil. Take one small roll for any length trip. Use as little as possible.

Markers. One permanent, waterproof marker is handy to have along for any number of uses.

Toilet paper. I've found better quality toilet paper goes farther than cheaper brands. One roll is usually ample for twelve to fifteen people per day—unless a case of diarrhea hits your camp.

Clorox II. For use in the porta-potty. Sprinkle in liberally. It keeps methane gas from building up and is relatively harmless.

Packing Methods and Equipment

Here it is the day before put-in, and the shopping crew has just returned with more food than you've ever seen outside a grocery store. The task of figuring out the best way to pack it seems monumental. The longer the trip, the more monstrous it can become. You may understandably be asking: "Now that I have it, what do I do with it?"

The solution—various waterproof boxes and bags—should be relatively easy to come by. The best waterproof containers are army surplus ammunition boxes. For years, Uncle Sam has provided all sorts of suitable equipment, most of it made to store bombs, missiles, and shells. For our purposes they have been converted to carrying food which may cause heartburn, indigestion, or cramps, but rarely death.

These military boxes vary greatly in size and shape. Ammo boxes most readily available range from small sizes of 10 inches long by 3⅞ inches wide by 6⅞ inches high and 11 by 5½ by 6⅞ to medium sizes of 11 by 5½ by 9¾ inches and 11 by 5½ by 12¼ and a large can measuring 17⅛ by 7½ by 13¼. Occasionally, even larger ammo boxes can be found. Two very desirable sizes are the long, narrow rocket box measuring 20 by 11 by 10½ inches and the cubical generator box measuring 17 by 17½ by 20. Other shapes and sizes can often be found at surplus stores and stores specializing in river equipment. Ammo boxes may be used for food, commissary items, pumps, first aid, cameras, and personal gear. Those with watertight lids will protect even your most delicate belongings.

To test a box for tightness, put water in it, clamp it shut, hold the box upside down, and inspect for leakage. (I've found the store's bathroom a suitable test lab.) If a box is fairly tight but not entirely waterproof, you may still want to consider it. While it may take on water in a wrap or flip, it will keep out rain and even heavy water coming over the side of the boat. For both occasional trips and frequent river running, ammunition boxes are worth the investment and the time spent searching for them.

Coolers are also quite useful for river trips. They make it possible to take perishable foods on the river that might otherwise be left behind. While coolers will fill up with water in a wrap or flip, a good cooler will keep out rain and water splashing over the side of the boat. Always tie a line over the top of a cooler to keep the lid from opening accidentally. I've found Rubbermaid brand Gott coolers to be far superior to other brands. They are extremely rugged, well insulated, and come in a large variety of sizes.

Wooden boxes can be used for the commissary, and boaters often custom-make one for this purpose. Metal footlockers can also be used for commissary and other items that do not have to remain perfectly dry. Surplus stores carry a selection of metal and sometimes wooden boxes.

Duffel bags are also useful for food storage, especially canned goods. A duffel lined with a heavy-duty plastic garbage bag will enable you to carry produce or personal gear when nothing else is available. Needless to say, in heavy rain or large white water your gear may get wet in a duffel.

While waterproof bags are best kept for personal clothing and sleeping gear, they can be used for food if necessary. Bakery products, paper products, noodles, rice, and flour could be stored in a waterproof bag.

With boxes lined up and food piled high, you're ready to start packing. At this point, you may prefer to start screaming. Don't let it overwhelm you. Relax, spread out, take your time, and enjoy yourself.

As with almost everything else, packing food can be done in a number of ways. If you're going out for a few days with a couple of friends, all your food will probably fit in one or two boxes or bags. Packing for an overnight trip, even with a large group, doesn't require much organization since you're not gone long enough to lose anything. For a canoe trip of a few days' length, packing will have to be concise and is therefore not complicated either. Longer raft trips are another story, however, and require a more involved packing arrangement.

If you've decided to use a daily menu or the cook's choice menu, you may also pack food by day, putting dinner, the following day's breakfast, and lunch in one box. (Keep the menu handy while packing.) You can easily take this one box off the boat, which eliminates extra unloading, makes all your ingredients easy to find, saves time when cooking, and immediately opens up a box for garbage. You can still use this scheme even if some food must be kept in coolers. There is no question that this is the most organized way to pack food, but if boxes vary greatly in volume, this arrangement could be difficult to use. This does not mean, however, that you must resort to haphazard packing, for there are other ways to maintain organization.

If you have a few large boxes rather than a number of smaller ones, you

can pack food by meals instead of by day. Breakfast foods would be packed together as would lunches and then dinners. If you have an item such as potatoes that you're using for both breakfast and dinner, divide the appropriate amount between the two boxes.

If you don't want to unload your boat every day, tie boxes by their handles so lids may be removed and food reached without untying the load.

This type of packing is also appropriate for long canoe trips with a number of canoes and will make everything easier to find.

When trips are lengthy and large quantities of food must be stored, packing by meal or day is simply not practical. For long trips, you will need to sort food by type. For example, rice, millet, and noodles might be packed together, as would cheeses or canned goods. This plan is especially useful when food must be separated due to perishability or when boxes and bags vary greatly in size.

Careful packing is crucial on any trip, and its importance increases with the length of the trip. If canned goods are stored on top of melons, for example, you'll have fruit salad before you are ready for it. Or, if potatoes are put in a leaky box, you may be able to distill your own vodka within a week. Perishable foods must be checked frequently to avoid losing the entire cache to mold. When packing canned goods in duffel bags, remove labels first since they come off in pieces when they get wet. To avoid having mystery ingredients, write the contents on the end of each can with indelible ink.

At times it will be necessary to transfer food from its original packaging to other containers. Packing food in a plastic bag rather than a box, or mixing dry ingredients for cakes and pancakes ahead of time can be real space savers. If food is purchased in bulk form, it may be safer and easier to carry split between a number of containers. Foods such as milk powder and flour that come in paper or cardboard wrappings are often better transferred to a plastic or metal container to keep them from getting damp. (Save yogurt cartons, honey jars, coffee cans, and similar containers for this purpose.)

No matter how organized you may be there are often miscellaneous items left over. You'll have to put them wherever they fit, which can make them difficult to find later. It's a familiar lament: "I know I packed it. . . ." On one- or two-day trips this is not a serious problem, but on longer trips something could stay lost for quite awhile.

There are two simple solutions to this problem. The first entails putting duct tape on a box and writing down the contents. This is especially convenient with a daily packing plan and packing by meal, since only the day number or type of meal must be written down. Duct tape leaves a mess on boxes, however, and even indelible pens fade from too much water and sun.

Another solution is especially useful for long trips with a large quantity of food. It will be joyfully received by those who are list fanatics. Paint a name on each box—trees, flowers, famous personalities, whatever. Jot the name of the box and its contents down on a piece of paper, along with whose boat it is on, place this list with the menu, and voilà—everything is instantly (well, almost) at your fingertips. This also works if boxes, bags, and coolers are distinctly different from one another. All you have to do is saunter down to the boats and select the proper groceries for the chosen recipe. Your arrangement might look like the following:

Patch's Boat
    Red cooler—cheese, yogurt, cream cheese, butter
    Green duffel—garbanzos, peas, applesauce
    Oscar Wilde—noodles, rice, millet

Steve's Boat
    Juniper—sunflower seeds, cashews, raisins
    Goofy—crackers, peanut butter, honey, jam
    Margarita—potatoes, carrots, onions

Occasionally some confusion may arise, but it won't last long and nothing will be lost—unless, of course, you lose the list!

Perishable Foods

While canned and dry goods make up a large part of river recipes, it is not necessary to do without fresh foods or dairy products, even on long trips. All vegetables will survive up to three days and many will last much longer. The more delicate ones incude broccoli, mushrooms, spinach, and lettuce. It is best to plan to use these vegetables before the fourth night, though occasionally they will last longer. Eggplant, Italian zucchini, scallions, and radishes may be served as late as the fifth night. Summer squash, green peppers, cucumbers, cauliflower, green beans, and celery will last over a week with proper care. Iceberg lettuce and tomatoes sometimes go bad within days and other times last for weeks. It seems to depend upon how fresh and firm they are when you buy them. Red and green cabbages, onions, carrots, and potatoes will last a month or more if packed properly.

Most fruit is generally not as durable as vegetables, but there are exceptions. Oranges can withstand an amazing amount of abuse and will usually last over three weeks. Apples, lemons, grapefruit, pineapple, and melons are also hardy and will often last well over a week. Avocados ripen after they are picked. The harder they are when you buy them, the longer they'll last, but a week is about maximum. Most other fruit will last only a few days, but for one- or two-day trips your selection is unlimited.

The greatest enemies of produce are mold and bruising. While shopping, select very fresh vegetables and firm, slightly unripe pieces of fruit. It helps to put fruit and vegetables in paper bags rather than plastic, since paper absorbs moisture that develops. It is important to keep fruit and vegetables dry and fairly cool because water and heat will cause them to rot. Watertight ammo boxes using the evaporative cooling system described below are invaluable for this purpose. If your cooler has space, produce will stay fresher on ice, though meat and dairy products should take precedence. Produce stored in ammo boxes must be checked daily for mold. If pieces have gone bad, throw them out. In a desert climate, produce may be aired at night so the dry air can absorb moisture. Spoilage will be less of a problem in cool weather than in hot, but produce should still be checked regularly.

Many dairy products are surprisingly durable. I've had yogurt, cream cheese, hard cheeses, and eggs remain fresh for more than four weeks. Butter, margarine, and sour cream will last two or three weeks. Milk and cream won't last more than a few days, however, even on ice. Powdered milk is a good substitute, though there is no real substitute for fresh cream. All dairy products must be kept cool to keep them from spoiling.

Meat, chicken, and fish should be frozen before the trip and stored directly on ice. Don't take chances with them: once spoiled, meat, fish, and poultry can cause serious illness. With a good cooler, meat will remain fresh three to five days, occasionally longer. If your cooling system is at all doubtful, substitute canned meat for fresh.

Other commonly used products that spoil easily are mayonnaise, tortillas, and bread. Mayonnaise should be kept cool after it has been opened. In hot weather, it is better not to save opened mayonnaise. You'll have less waste if you purchase eight-ounce jars, even though they are more expensive than larger sizes. Salads mixed with mayonnaise and allowed to stand in the heat a number of hours can cause food poisoning. Those containing meat or fish are especially dangerous—leftovers should be thrown away. Tortillas are easy to carry but generally begin to mold after about five days. On warm-weather trips, bread will often last about a week, and I've had it stay fresh for a month on one cool weather trip. Bread is bulky, though, and may require more space than you have available. Crackers are good substitutes and last indefinitely. Camp-made tortillas, homemade bread, and biscuits will also add variety to the menu. While whole eggs keep well, powdered eggs can be a real space-saver on long trips. Use powdered eggs for baking and mixing in batters and keep fresh eggs for omelets.

Perishable foods may be kept fresh in one of two ways. The most obvious method is storing food in a cooler with block ice. A ten-pound block of ice may last from three to ten days. In order for ice to survive, a cooler must be well insulated, carried low in the boat, opened infrequently, closed tightly after removing something, and covered with a wet cloth to prevent the sun from heating it. Drain ice water out of a cooler regularly so food doesn't get wet. Because of their insulating qualities, coolers become very hot once the ice has melted. At that point, they are best used for transporting garbage, since they are worthless for food.

The ancient cooling system of evaporation is a very effective alternative to ice and is ideal for use with ammo boxes. Furthermore, the main ingredient is flowing by your fingertips. This method can be used for produce and dairy products but not meat. After packing, close boxes tightly and position together on one boat. Take a heavyweight cloth—terry towels or burlap bags are most suitable—and wet thoroughly. Lay cloth across boxes, and as it dries, rewet it. The evaporation of the water will keep the temperature of the box and food inside below fifty degrees Fahrenheit. (Metal boxes are better than plastic because they chill better.) Place these boxes underneath other gear to prevent the sun from heating them. Evaporative cooling is a favorite of mine, and I have used it on long trips with great success.

Dry ice is another option, though it could be considered a luxury item. It is quite expensive, and if used in place of block ice will not last much longer; but dry ice will keep food frozen solid. This is beneficial for meat and frozen juices since it extends the length of time they may be carried. In addition, block ice can be stored with dry ice and used to replenish other coolers.

Specialized Plans for Particular Boaters

In the preceding sections, I went into great detail on how to plan and pack for trips lasting from one day to one month, provided you have the equipment to carry everything. If you are a canoeist, kayaker, or a beginning rafter without much gear, your packing needs are a little more specialized.

Two in a Canoe

Canoeing one of the many rivers in this country can be an idyllic vacation. Though canoeists cannot carry the bulk that rafters often (by choice) carry, they can still enjoy almost all the recipes in this book. Your key to success lies in organizing your planning and packing before the trip. Measure out exact amounts of ingredients at home and put them in Ziploc bags, squeeze-tube containers designed for backpackers, and small jars. To conserve even more space, make some dishes at home, place them in plastic containers, store in your cooler, and reheat once you're on the river. Spices and herbs can be stored handily in small plastic bags or 35mm film containers.

Utensils designed for backpackers will enable you to carry a complete mess kit without the weight of cast iron or stainless steel. Baking does not have to be forgone either since small, cast-aluminum Dutch ovens are easy for a canoeist to carry. When planning your menu, take your route into consideration. If you'll have a number of portages, plan simple, lightweight meals and save the more elaborate dishes for an easier trip, or when there are a number of people to help prepare the recipe.

Care and Feeding of Kayakers

Proper care and feeding of the kayaker is no easy task. Slithering around in a second rubberized skin, shelled head, and with an elongated growth at their waists, they frequently have a gaunt and hungry appearance and a crazed look in their eyes. Kayakers probably expend more energy than other boaters but are more difficult to feed because they are essentially the back packers of the river world and are obliged to travel light. However, overnight trips without raft support are possible. Special float bags designed to carry gear along with necessary flotation are being produced. You can also use two heavy-duty garbage bags placed inside a nylon stuff sack.

Since the ties that come with the bags can poke holes in the bag and do not close it tightly enough, close the bag with an overhand knot. While garbage bags last only one or two days before developing pinhole leaks, float bags cost considerably more and may last only six or seven trips. There are limitations, of course, as to the length of a trip, unless you wish to emulate two men I know who survived eight days on hard-cooked eggs and candy bars while doing a winter Grand Canyon trip. For the more sensible, here are some menu suggestions.

Breakfasts: Hot and cold cereals, and powdered or freeze-dried eggs will give you some variety. Add onions and cheese to the latter for flavor and leave yogurt out of cereal. To prevent scurvy add the ever durable orange to your diet. Apples, while not as sturdy as oranges, can be taken on short trips as well. Instant coffee, tea, or cereal beverage will finish out your morning meal.

Lunches: Grand Canyon Gorp could be the most valuable food you carry. It is high in carbohydrates, full of energy, and tastes good. Peanut butter and jam sandwich is another favorite. The proportions recommended to me by John Cassidy (author of *A Peanut Butter Journal,* an account of a twelve-day kayaking trip) are six parts peanut butter to four parts jam. He recommends making the sandwiches at home or in camp and carrying them in the bread bag. If you're going out just for the day, you can make any of the lunches in the book. Since most contain mayonnaise, store the sandwich in the bottom of the kayak so it will stay cool. Second-day lunches should leave out garnish items like celery, green pepper, pickle relish, black olives, and water chestnuts to save weight.

Dinners: Drifter's Onion Soup and Hermit Creek Potato Soup can be followed exactly. Noodle-Cheese-Nut Thing needs some alteration by using envelopes of cream of mushroom soup rather than cans and mixing at half strength. For additional protein and flavor, add tuna, bonito, or salmon. Simple Spaghetti from Scratch is another easy dish. Make sauce at home and for more protein add ground beef to the recipe. You can make Beans Amandine as well by using fresh green beans and envelopes of cream of mushroom soup, mixing at half strength. If you make Sierra Foothills Pottage, Cabbage Onion Soup, and many of the vegetable stews and casseroles in the Vegie Delights section at home, put them in a plastic container and freeze so you can have delicious meals that can be carried easily in your kayak. Other dinners suggested by kayakers include Rice-a-Roni, Top Ramen Noodles, and freeze-dried foods.

Packing, of course, is very important. All ingredients must be measured at home and only the exact amount taken. Store things in Ziploc bags and squeeze-tube containers designed for backpackers. Your utensils can be cut to a minimum and need only include one pot, a cutting knife, spoon, cup, and eating utensils.

The Duffel Bag Special

One of the great pleasures of boating is spending time with your friends around a campfire while the voice of the river sings to you. If you're a beginning rafter and haven't accumulated a great deal of gear, don't put off an overnight trip. While waterproof boxes and bags are invaluable, you can still carry gear without them and keep everything relatively dry, with nothing more than a couple of duffel bags. You are limited to a two-, or possibly a three-day trip at the most, but with careful packing you can do that overnight trip.

Choose recipes with the most durable foods: canned goods, hot and cold cereals, Bisquick, macaroni and rice dishes, cheeses, even eggs if you have a plastic case to carry them in. Stay away from breads and fresh fruit and vegetables with the exception of: potatoes, onions, cabbages, carrots, oranges, and apples. Assuming you don't even have a cooler, meat can still be carried if it is frozen, wrapped in newspaper, and put in a heavy-duty plastic bag.

At least two duffels, one for canned goods and utensils, the other for dry foods, produce, dairy, and spices, will be necessary. Make use of all sorts of plastic containers and seal them shut with duct tape or they are liable to decorate everything else in the bag with their contents. You might also put staple items such as oil, vinegar, milk powder, and honey in small plastic containers before starting out. Pack each meal separately and tightly in small cardboard boxes. Line the duffel with a plastic bag and put cardboard boxes inside. Store frozen meat with canned goods so it does not damage the produce or dry food as it melts. Be sure to tie everything down well and don't step on the bags or put heavy objects on top of fragile ones. With care, your food will remain intact, as long as you don't flip or wrap.

Utensils, Staples, Spices and Herbs

Even overnight trips require cooking utensils, some staple items, and a selection of spices. On short trips, all three may be condensed into one box, or even combined with food. Long expeditions usually require three separate containers.

Utensils

The utensils you select for your trip will be determined by your carrying capacity and your menu. Canoeists will do well with a set of pots designed for backpackers, while rafters may want to take a fuller selection. An enamelware coffee pot is ideal and cast iron, if you don't mind the weight, is wonderful for griddles, frying pans, and Dutch ovens. Bargain shoppers will find thrift stores a good source of kitchen items. They should be kept clean and reasonably dry and might include some or all of the following:

Camp-style coffee pot
Frying pan or griddle
Mixing bowl(s)
Cutting knives
Measuring cups
Can opener
Vegetable steamer
Grater
Corkscrew
Tea ball
Strainer
Potholders
Channel-lock pliers
Charcoal lighter fluid
Dutch oven(s)
Nesting pots

Spoons: serving, slotted, wooden,
    measuring
Cutting board
Spatula(s)
Wire whip
Tongs
Plates, bowls, cups
Aluminum pie plate(s)
Knives, forks, spoons
Matches
Dish pails
Dish soap, scrubber, sponges
Fire pan and grate (these would be
    packed separately from utensils
    but are an integral part of the
    river kitchen)

Staples

Staples are items used frequently though intermittently, with or between meals. They should be packed tightly in a dry box. The basics include:

Flour
Baking powder
Baking soda
Tamari or soy sauce
Worcestershire sauce
River Runners' Recipes
    or menu cards
Coffee
Tea
Hot chocolate

Honey
Sugar
Dry milk
Matches
Ketchup
Mustard
Aluminum foil
Plastic garbage bags
Paper towels
Freezer or Ziploc bags

Spices and Herbs

Spices and herbs are those aromatic substances that enhance flavors and change a dull dish into an exciting entrée. You'll want to experiment with choices and amounts as you become familiar with the recipes and with your own tastes. The following list of spices and herbs includes those most frequently used in the recipes in this book.

Salt	Turmeric	Rosemary
Black pepper	Basil	Dry mustard
Garlic powder	Thyme	Chili powder
Onion powder	Oregano	Cayenne pepper
Cinnamon	Parsley	Vanilla
Curry powder	Tarragon	Dill seed
Cumin	Nutmeg	Celery seed
Ginger	Cloves	Sage
Paprika	Bay leaves	

With the basics behind you, it is time to depart. Boats are loaded, paddles and oars are in hand. All that is left is the pleasure of flowing with the river. Enjoy, and eat hearty!

SETTING
UP
CAMP

After a long day on the river, an overnight camp is a welcome sight. While you want your camp to be comfortable and convenient, certain rules of etiquette are advisable. On some popular rivers I've seen fierce competition over campsites, which strikes me as in sad contrast to the essence of river running. When traveling a popular river, check with other parties about their plans for camp and let them know yours. If the river is new to your party, you may also obtain information about camps from other boaters. If your party is small, don't take a big campsite that a larger group might need.

Essential to any camp is an acceptable place to dock boats, with a sturdy tree or rock available for tying them. If a beach offers nothing but five hundred yards of sand, a "deadman" can be improvised. Tie one end of a line securely to a sturdy log and leave the other end of the line free. Dig a two-foot hole in the sand and bury the log, leaving the free end of the line out. After testing for strength, tie boats securely to this line. Make sure the "deadman" is above the high water mark and be aware on all rivers of the fluctuation possibilities: you don't want to wake up in the morning and find your boats missing. Whenever possible, choose a campsite with a kitchen site close to the boats so that unloading and loading is relatively easy. With large parties, this can be facilitated by forming a human chain and passing gear along the length of it.

Give some consideration to the arrangement of your camp. A secluded location is necessary for the porta-potty, level sites free of rocks and tree roots are desirable for sleeping, and the relationship of your work space to the fire is important. In a river canyon, for example, winds usually blow upstream during the afternoon and early evening before dying down at night, so if you arrange your camp accordingly you can avoid working in a smoke screen.

During rainy weather a dry kitchen will add considerably to your comfort. A well-erected tarp can create a cozy atmosphere, enabling you to enjoy dinner in warm, dry clothes while the storm rages around you. Trees, oars, paddles, boulders, and logs can serve as corner posts to hold a tarp aloft, and lines will hold it in place. A tarp should be high enough to stand under and sturdy enough to withstand the wind that often accompanies rain.

Tie a line to each corner of the tarp. If your tarp does not have grommets, put a small stone in the corner and fold the edges of the tarp around it. Next, tie the lines to four stationary points. When using oars or paddles as corner posts, put them blade down into the dirt or sand and lean the oar away from the tarp. Tie the tarp line to the oar or paddle handle, along with two loose lines. Run these lines to large rocks on the ground and position the rocks to form a triangle with the blade. With taut lines and heavy rocks, this system will work even with oars at all four points. While paddles are too short to be used all around, they may be used at one end to create a lean-to. Put the low end into the wind. Station one or two props under the center of the tarp to provide drainage and prevent rainwater from collecting in one spot. Arrange kitchen gear around these posts if possible, so people won't knock them down. Place a fire at the downwind end of the tarp so it is sheltered slightly but doesn't take up all the dry space and so that sparks won't burn the tarp.

A table might be considered an unnecessary luxury until you realize how easy it is to carry one on a raft, drift boat, or dory. Having a table makes meal preparation easier and keeps food free of sand and dirt. A deck taken off a raft and placed between two ammo boxes makes an instant table. Keep a deck free for this use by loading it with things that come off the boat daily, such as kitchen equipment or personal bags. For the convenience of a standard-height table, outfit a deck with floor flanges and buy threaded pipe in two- or three-foot lengths to serve as legs. In place of a table, covers from ammo boxes, a top of a cooler, or a tablecloth can provide clean, usable work space.

Once a kitchen has been established, set up a hand-wash. This can be a bucket of water with a bar of soap next to it or a special canteen with a spigot. The hand-wash should be used before touching any food, which can do a lot to keep a group healthy. Obviously anyone with an infection or a cold should stay away from food preparation.

Another valuable kitchen item is the bailer—the three- to five-gallon white plastic bucket used for bailing water out of a boat. A bailer filled with water can be used for a hand-wash, washing fruit and vegetables, settling silty water, and chilling wine, beer, or other drinks. Clean bailers will serve as salad bowls or drink containers, and are also practical for transporting food between rafts and kitchen. A bailer can be adapted as a garbage container by putting a plastic bag inside it and folding the bag over the edge of the bucket. Filled with sand and buried, a bailer can serve as a "deadman" anchor for boats, volleyball nets, and rainy day tarps. Designate bailers for specific jobs to avoid putting food in one that had soap in it the night before. You can often obtain bailers from restaurants and stores since most of their bulk food comes in these buckets.

In order to discourage nocturnal visitors, return leftover food and staples to coolers and boxes before going to bed. Store garbage in the utensils box and clamp or tie all lids on tightly. If your food is in bags, tie them from tree limbs. Wild animals have become quite clever at opening boxes and getting into the food supply, but a few pots and pans piled on top of boxes at night will scare them off if they then become too persistent. While feeding wild animals is tempting, this does them a disservice since they then become dependent upon human food. They can also become a nuisance, and in the case of bears can pose some danger.

Water Purification

Fewer and fewer rivers are potable these days and some method of dealing with this dilemma is a necessary part of your river trip. It is wise not to trust any river unless you know it well. A crystal-clear stream may be polluted, while a muddy one could be relatively clean.

One method that ensures good-tasting, clean water is to carry it from home in five-gallon jugs. Provided you have the raft space, this can be done even on longer trips, and is common on desert rivers where streams are silty and carry some pollution.

Some rivers may have clean side creeks, and these can be used to replenish your supply. When these are plentiful and reliable, you need only carry one or two five-gallon jugs to insure you always have clean water.

When it is necessary to purify water, water filters are definitely the best method as they do not use chemicals or affect the taste. Katadyn manufactures a state-of-the-art filter with an accompanying price tag. First Need has a deluxe filter for less, but the filter will need replacing more often than Katadyn's.

As far as chemical disinfectants go, the two most popular I've encountered are chlorine and iodine. The former is easily obtained by buying a bottle of Clorox and adding eight drops per gallon of water. Allow the mixture to stand for half an hour before drinking. For large quantities of water, iodine crystals are the most economical. R.E.I. carries a kit with instructions for use in its catalog. Adding a powdered drink mix or some lemon slices to the treated water will help kill the chemical taste.

When traveling on silt-laden rivers, allow water to stand undisturbed overnight in bailing buckets so the silt can settle to the bottom of the container. In the morning, filter or chemically treat the settled water.

Campfires and Stoves

The campfire: that friendly glow in the night; the warmth that takes away the chill; the entity that creates the atmosphere.

A safe, practical place to contain a campfire is the first prerequisite. This place should be sheltered enough to prevent wind from scattering embers and starting a forest or brush fire, and should also provide support for a grate. Many river camps have an existing firepit. Use it! Too frequently there is more than one. To help preserve the natural environment, this second (or third) firepit could be broken apart and cleaned up. If there is no existing firepit when you arrive at camp, break apart and clean up yours when leaving the following morning.

On many rivers under the jurisdiction of the Park Service or Bureau of Land Management, you are required to carry a firepan. Some people regard this as another restriction on their freedom, but using a firepan is a sound ecological practice. A firepan prevents soot and ashes from leaving ugly scars at campsites and is additional protection against forest and brush fires.

Practical firepans can be made out of a number of heavy-duty metal items. With a simple alteration, a large, galvanized washtub (about twenty-two-inch top diameter) makes one of the best firepans I've ever used. Cut a hole in the side of the tub between the seams with a hacksaw. This gives the fire additional air and makes it accessible when a grate and pots cover the top of the pan. Leave the rim on the pan to give it extra strength and make the hole about eight by seventeen inches, large enough for a medium-size log to pass through. The tub is deep, so even a strong breeze won't blow the fire around, and is large enough to effectively contain a substantial campfire. With a grate on top, there is enough room for a few pots. The tub also has handles, making it easy to tie down on a raft or dory. Because of its size, however, it is not practical for canoes or very small rafts.

If you require a smaller firepan, consider a garbage can lid or metal oil-pan. For cooking purposes, you'll need a grate with legs, since these pans are too shallow to put a grate on top of them. If you do your cooking on a stove but like a campfire for warmth or atmosphere, these two are quite suitable and are easily carried, even in a small boat.

A truly deluxe firepan can be made from an oil drum by an experienced welder. Have the drum cut in half lengthwise with a blowtorch. Each half will resemble a cradle. Only one half is needed for the firepan. Have one end cut down to provide access to the fire, leaving a two- or three-inch lip at the bottom to prevent ashes from falling out. Next, weld angle iron around the top three edges and across the open end. This will keep the firepan from warping and will smooth out rough edges. Have legs welded on the bottom of the pan to steady it, or support it firmly with rocks before using. This size firepan is suited to large groups with large boats who do most or all of their cooking over a fire. If you decide to have a drum converted into a firepan, make sure it did not originally contain a flammable substance or it could explode when cut with a blowtorch.

With all firepans, put a layer of sand in the bottom of the pan before building a fire to keep the fire from burning through the metal.

Building a campfire is an art in itself. Consider carefully the safety of the location, especially when using a firepit. Build a fire on sand, hard dirt, or gravel, but never on grass or against a dead tree or log. Placing a fire next to boulders or rock walls should be avoided as well, for smoke will blacken them. Never leave a fire unattended, even for a short time.

When traveling a popular river, it is a good idea to begin collecting wood before reaching camp. Places along shore with no campsites provide a good source of deadwood. Putting wood on top of gear or in a tarp in the bottom of the boat will get it to camp dry—as long as this is done after the last big rapid.

Choose small branches rather than large logs for firewood. There is usually no need to build a large blaze and then let it die down to cook over coals. That method might be useful when preparing meals for groups of twenty or more, or when barbecuing meat, but otherwise a large fire is a waste of time and wood. With the increased use of our waterways, it is wise to practice firewood conservation. Deadwood provides fertilizer for a forest floor and homes for small animals, so don't burn it unnecessarily. Finally, large logs create a lot of smoke which has a nasty habit of following *you* around.

Start a fire by using paper, dried grass, or pine needles as a base, then add half a dozen small, dry branches. Place kindling in a crisscross or tent shape so air may circulate. Light the kindling, and as the flame grows add more branches. Continue to add one stick at a time to regulate heat. If a fire is maintained with small pieces of wood, up to an inch in diameter, the heat can be controlled as effectively as on a stove. In addition, a grate placed across a firepan provides a level cooking surface and allows pots to be moved around for further control of heat while cooking.

Starting a fire in wet weather can certainly be difficult, but is not impossible. Look for dry branches underneath trees or covered by leaves and pine needles. Build up a kindling base and douse with charcoal lighter fluid. Wait about five minutes to allow fluid to penetrate wood. Light kindling and add more wood, using smaller branches than usual. Dry out additional wood by placing it next to the fire or around the edges of the grate.

The temperature of a fire will vary with the amount and kind of wood used. Hard woods burn hotter and cleaner than soft woods. On a river, however, often there is no choice as only driftwood is available. Learning to recognize a low, medium, or hot fire won't take long. Watch the dish that is cooking closely, and it will indicate the temperature of the fire quite accurately.

Always douse a fire thoroughly when finished with it and dispose of ashes appropriately. On many rivers, ashes may be dumped in the fast-moving current after picking out large pieces that will not sink. When you are required to carry ashes out, smother them with water. Allow hot coals to cool, then shovel into a plastic garbage bag. If at any time you come upon a firepit filled with ashes and trash, pack this debris out in a garbage bag. When a permit is required, specific details on the use of fire and disposal of ashes will be included. These are not idle rules made to encumber you with unnecessary work, but part of a careful consideration of that particular ecology.

In many instances, a stove is far more practical than a campfire. Pots stay cleaner, wood does not have to be collected, and the temperature is easier to regulate. On the other hand, stoves are cumbersome to carry, must be kept relatively dry, and are more expensive to operate than a fire. In some areas wood is very scarce, however, and other places, such as the Grand Canyon, have strict limitations on the use of wood. In these instances a stove is a prerequisite for making the trip.

Two types of stoves are used most frequently for river running. One uses white gas or unleaded fuel and the other uses propane. A three-burner stove is most practical for large commercial trips, while a two-burner will probably suit trips of up to twelve people. The cost of both types of stoves and fuels is roughly the same, and each has advantages and disadvantages.

Propane is easier to use than white gas. The latter must be pumped and cleaned regularly, while a propane bottle is hooked up to a stove and a valve turned on. Propane is safer, since there is always a danger of gasoline catching fire or exploding. Occasionally, however, a valve on a propane bottle will leak and a few weeks' fuel supply could be lost in a matter of days. Both fuels come in small quantities, making them easy to store and enabling you to buy only what you need. If you decide to use propane and you take frequent overnight trips, you might want to consider a five-gallon propane tank. While the larger tank can be awkward to carry, you will save money. (Never store any fuel in a food box; the smell will remain in the box and permeate everything.)

Even if you plan to cook over a fire your entire trip, carry a small stove as a backup. If wood is scarce or is soaked by days of rain, your stove can mean the difference between having hot meals or cold. Small one-burner stoves do not require much storage space and are also handy to have along for overnight side hikes.

Dishwashing and Sanitation

An important part of the kitchen equipment will be one or more "chickie" pails (a name derived from the multibucket hot water system used to defrock chickens). For our purposes, a chickie pail is a fairly large, galvanized bucket used for dishwashing. Put chickie pails on to boil as soon as a fire is started. If you place three or four glowing charcoal briquets under each pail, the water will remain hot for hours.

Small parties can have a simple dishwashing system by heating one chickie pail and distributing hot water between it and a bailing bucket for a soapy wash and clear rinse.

A system of four chickie pails is desirable for groups of ten or more and is frequently used by commercial outfitters. This method includes two soapy washes: the first turns a murky gray from food particles, while the second does the actual cleaning. The third bucket is a clear, hot rinse. The last bucket is a clear, cold rinse with a few drops of Clorox added to disinfect dishes. Allow dishes to sit in the final bucket three to five minutes for the Clorox to be effective. The Clorox smell and taste will disappear as dishes are aired on a draining board. While a second soapy wash may sometimes be eliminated, it is always wise to have a Clorox rinse on any long, very isolated trip or with a large group of people. In a remote canyon, any sickness or injury becomes intensified. Gastrointestinal illness is a common river affliction and a small precaution such as this could help prevent illness from spreading.

If you want to keep your pots from becoming sooty, smear a thin layer of dishsoap over the pot before putting it on the fire. The soot will then come off easily in the wash (a good reason to save those pots for last). This is especially useful for an occasional trip using home utensils. For those river rats who do numerous trips, a separate set of river equipment is advisable.

There is always the temptation, of course, to do away with elaborate dishwashing systems and clean dishes in the river. This may have a primitive appeal, but will not result in clean dishes. Hot water and soap are necessary to cut grease and reduce the risk of passing illness through the group. Furthermore, negligent cleaning methods leave behind food particles which attract insects and animals. This can cause some distress if you stumble over a skunk or are stung by a fire ant.

Garbage should always be carried out. Place a garbage bag at the head of the chickie pail line so food scraps can be dumped in it. In a forest canyon, dig a hole off to one side of the camp and pour dirty water through a strainer into this sump. In the desert, where nothing decomposes quickly and the rivers have a much greater volume than mountain rivers have, pour dishwater through a strainer into a bailing bucket. Load the dirty water onto a boat and dump it into the fast-moving current of the river. In both cases, the strainer is emptied into the garbage bag. Burying organic waste is not an acceptable alternative. Animals will uncover it, and on a popular river it is possible to dig up other burial sites, giving your trip the quality of an archaeological expedition.

Proper disposal of garbage is often the most neglected aspect of a trip. It seems so inconsequential to toss it, and much easier than looking for a strainer or putting out a garbage bag. But our wilderness areas are dwindling and it is important to take care of them. Those who leave garbage behind are lazy, do not know better, or simply don't care—about the river, the land, or other people. Before leaving any camp, go over it thoroughly and pick up pull-tabs, cigarette butts, and other trash so you can help leave that wilderness canyon looking like a wilderness.

The Dutch Oven

Any river trip can be improved by the addition of freshly baked quiche, casseroles, and cakes. Newcomers to river travel are always amazed and often perplexed as to how such a feat is managed so far from a home oven. When they are shown the Dutch oven that produced the savory dish, their surprise grows. But Dutch oven cookery is really quite simple, and the gratification that comes with producing luxurious meals is comparable to running a rapid well, making up with your lover, or watching a beautiful sunset. It is as difficult for me to imagine a river trip without a Dutch oven as it would be to imagine one without a raft, kayak, canoe, or peanut butter.

This ingeniously designed pot is a self-contained baking unit. Most Dutch ovens have three legs. Those that do not may be raised off the ground two inches with the help of small rocks. The cover must be flat, with a raised lip around the outside edge to contain coals. Dutch ovens are available in both cast iron and aluminum, but nothing can compare to the seasoning and cooking quality of cast iron. Aluminum does not heat as well and can melt if put directly on a hot fire. Dutch ovens can be purchased in surplus stores and variety shops carrying housewares. They usually come in diameter sizes from eight to sixteen inches. An eight-inch Dutch oven yields a cake large enough for ten people or a main course for three to five. A ten-inch Dutch oven provides an ample dinner for seven to ten people, and so on—up to a sixteen-inch Dutch oven, which will hold a dinner for twenty to twenty-five people.

Caring for your Dutch oven is a very personal matter. Traditionally, dirty dishes are washed in soapy water and this method will clean a Dutch oven effectively. Soap removes previous seasonings from cast iron, however, and it is these seasonings that keep food from sticking to the pot. Other cleaning methods involve some creativity. Use salt as an abrasive to loosen particles of

food, or heat oil in the oven and scrape clean with a spatula. Or pour a thin layer of wine or other alcoholic beverage into the oven and heat for a few minutes to loosen stuck food. If this isn't enough, use plain boiling water and a scrubber to loosen charred particles. Clear water will not wash away previous seasonings. After rinsing the Dutch oven, place it over a low fire to dry completely and then reseason. It is imperative that cast iron be dried thoroughly and oiled before being put away, or you may end up with a rusty pot.

Preheat a Dutch oven by oiling it well and placing the pot and cover at the edge of the fire. When the ingredients are ready, put them directly inside the oven. Cover, and set on a flat spot that has been selected ahead of time. (There is nothing worse than being all ready and suddenly realizing you have no place to put your creation.) Flat rocks or hard-packed dirt are ideal surfaces. Avoid placing the oven in sand, as it will extinguish the coals, or on grass, as you may start a fire. Wind will cool a Dutch oven, so choose a sheltered spot if it is breezy. Before leaving camp, shovel the remains of the coals into a garbage bag.

Charcoal briquets are the best heating source for a Dutch oven. They are easy to carry, give off even, intense heat, and will remain hot long enough to bake a dish. If a campfire is burning, start briquets by placing them on a grate over the fire. Otherwise, place briquets in a pile, douse with lighter fluid, wait a few minutes for the fluid to saturate the briquets, and light with a match.

Once started, briquets will turn gray in ten to fifteen minutes and are then ready to use for baking. Timing is important. If briquets are started too early, they will expire before the dish is baked. *Never* start or use briquets in an enclosed space, since they are toxic and can cause asphyxiation.

When briquets are ready, transfer them to the Dutch oven with tongs. If your oven is some distance from the fire, a small tin plate is helpful to carry them over the intervening space. (Don't forget your potholder!) About two-thirds of the briquets will be placed on top of the oven, with the remainder underneath. Those underneath should be just within the outside edge, not bunched together but spread out, so the heat will radiate evenly. Those on top are placed around the outside edge of the cover against the lip, evenly spaced.

Avoid the temptation to lift the cover while the Dutch oven dish is baking, since you lose about ten minutes of cooking time each time you do this. You may also be tempted to use more coals than necessary the first couple of times, doubting that so few can do so much. The number of briquets and the baking times in the following recipes have been tested and will serve as a guide for other recipes you may wish to try. It is advisable, however, to heat a few more briquets than the recipe calls for in the event some are lost in the fire. As a rule, the baking time is slightly longer than in a home oven. Test with a knife or use the "nose" test. When you begin to smell the finished product, wait five or ten minutes, then check it. This test is highly accurate and your dish will usually be done. Good luck!

BEGINNING
THE DAY

Morning Crank

Yield: 6 cups
Preparation time: 25 minutes

The ritual of making camp coffee can sometimes be as important as the ingredients.

Water
Regular grind coffee   ⅔ cup
Eggshells
Lots of patience

Fill 2-quart coffeepot with cold water and place over a hot fire. When water boils, remove pot from fire and pour coffee into water. Place eggshells on top of grounds. (The calcium in eggshells absorbs the acid in coffee.) Gently submerge coffee and shells with a large spoon or by slowly swinging pot back and forth by its handle. Allow coffee to brew off the fire 5 minutes, then take 1 cup cold water and pour it slowly into coffee. (Cold water helps sink grounds to the bottom of the pot.) Again, allow it to sit 5 minutes off the fire. At last it is ready to serve! Place remaining coffee at edge of fire to keep warm, but do not let it boil or it will become bitter.

Rogue River Smoothie

Yield: 10-ounce glass
Preparation time: 10 minutes

The Rogue River area in southern Oregon is a bewitching place. The river flows between thick forests of conifer and oak, through a narrow canyon, and past open meadows and side creeks abounding with wildlife. The rapids are short, easy drops with the exception of Rainie Falls and Blossom Bar, which add a touch of excitement to every trip.

Milk powder   ¼ cup
Very cold water   1 cup
Fresh or canned fruit   ¼ cup
Plain or flavored yogurt   ¼ cup
Cinnamon and nutmeg   to taste

Mix milk powder with cold water. Dice fruit very small. Put all ingredients in 16-ounce jar, cover, shake vigorously, and pour into glass.

Any Ol' Time Fruit Salad

Serves 4 to 6
Preparation time: 30 minutes

This recipe is perfect for long trips as the ingredients will remain fresh for weeks. It is filling enough to be a meal in itself.

Red apples   4 medium, diced
Oranges   3, peeled and sectioned
Pitted dates   1 cup chopped
Raisins   1 cup
Figs   1 cup chopped
Any other available fruit
Walnuts   ½ cup chopped
Pineapple or cranberry juice   8-ounce can
Cinnamon and nutmeg   to taste
Plain yogurt   2 pounds

Combine first 10 ingredients in a bowl. Stir in yogurt. Or, leave fruit salad plain and serve yogurt on the side.

Shenandoah Fresh Fruit Salad

Serves 10
Preparation time: 30 minutes

The melodious sound of the name Shenandoah is only one facet of this river's beauty. Whether wandering through the Blue Ridge Mountains of Virginia or tumbling over the exciting Shenandoah Staircase near historic Harpers Ferry in West Virginia, the Shenandoah will charm boaters from eight to eighty.

Small bananas   7, peeled
Peaches   5, pitted
Pineapple   1, peeled and cored
Strawberries   1-pint box, hulled
Cantaloupe   1, peeled and seeded
Honeydew melon   1, peeled and seeded
Casaba melon   1, peeled and seeded
Cashews   1 cup
Plain yogurt   2 pounds

Cut fruit into bite-size pieces and combine in a bowl. Add cashews. Mix yogurt with fruit or serve on the side.

Potomac Granola and Fruit

Serves 8
Preparation time: 15 minutes

For those early morning departures or overnight hikes up side canyons, this breakfast is simple and provides excellent energy. George Washington's Potomac offers wild beauty within a short distance of the District of Columbia's monuments. The river also provides excellent boating for both beginning canoeists and advanced kayakers.

Milk powder   1½ cups
Cold water   4 cups
Granola   1½ pounds
Raisins, figs, dates   1 cup each, chopped
Plain yogurt   2 pounds

Combine milk powder with water, mixing thoroughly. Serve ingredients in any desired combination.

Early Morning Mix

Serves 6
Preparation time: 20 minutes

This breakfast is especially nice on a cold, rainy morning as it seems to heat up your entire body.

Water   4 cups
Salt   1 teaspoon
Cream of Wheat   ¾ cup
Cream of Rice   ¾ cup
Wheatena   ¾ cup
Honey and raisins   6 tablespoons each
Milk powder   ¾ cup
Water   3 cups
Plain yogurt   2 pounds

Bring salted water to boil. Reduce heat, add cereals, and cook over medium heat 5 minutes. Put 1 tablespoon of honey and handful of raisins in bottom of individual bowl. Pour hot cereal over honey and raisins, mixing well. Combine milk powder with water. Serve cereal topped with milk and yogurt.

Lisa's Millet Mix

Serves 6
Preparation time: 40 minutes

Boatwoman Lisa Nemzer has a good knowledge of nutrition. Her contribution of this recipe to a trip furnished a healthy and delicious breakfast—much to the surprise of the skeptics in the group.

Water   3 cups
Salt   ½ teaspoon
Millet   1 cup
Honey, raisins, and date bits   1 cup each
Milk powder   ¾ cup
Water   3 cups
Plain yogurt   2 pounds

Bring salted water to a boil. Add millet and cook about 30 minutes, or until all the water is absorbed. Mix honey, raisins, and date bits in with cooked millet. Combine milk powder with water and serve over cereal with yogurt.

Bacon and Sausage for a Bunch

Serves 6 to 20
Preparation time: 30 minutes

Cooking bacon or sausage for a group is not easily done in a frying pan or even on a large griddle. Here is an easy method that can be used for any amount of meat.

Bacon or sausage   1 to 3 pounds

Cover bottom of 3-gallon pot with ⅛ inch of water and add all bacon or sausage. Allow about ⅙ pound per person. Cover and bring water to a boil. Continue boiling 10 minutes, turning meat occasionally. Drain excess liquid into empty coffee can, mayonnaise jar, or other suitable container. Place uncovered pot back on fire and brown meat, stirring frequently, to keep from burning. As individual pieces of meat are done, transfer them with tongs to another pot lined with paper towels or napkins. Keep meat warm by placing pot at edge of fire.
Note: Do not pour grease into a sump hole, as it attracts insects and animals. Either carry it out or burn it in a hot fire, which makes for an easy, clean disposal.

Saint John Fried Potatoes

Serves 6
Preparation time: 45 minutes

Clamoring and sliding through the spruce and fir backwoods of northwestern Maine, the Saint John River offers a delightful springtime trip to canoeists and rafters. This is a fitting dish for the Saint John as the river flows through Aroostock County, an area known as the "potato empire of the world."

Medium potatoes   6
Medium yellow onion   1
Oil   ¼ to ½ cup
Black pepper, garlic powder, parsley flakes, and dill weed   1 teaspoon
    each

Wash potatoes in clear water. Cut potatoes in half, quarter each half, and thinly slice each quarter. Chop onion into small pieces. Coat a large frying pan or griddle with oil and heat over a medium fire. When oil is hot, add potatoes and cover. It is important to cover pan in order to fry potatoes without first boiling them. Cook slowly, turning occasionally. When potatoes are about half done, add onion, spices, and herbs. Fry until tender and brown. Serve hot.

Rio Grande Huevos Rancheros

Serves 6
Preparation time: 30 minutes

As the Rio Grande forms the border between Texas and Mexico, it flows through the deep canyons of Big Bend National Park and a section known as Lower Canyons. Tales of rattlesnakes, quicksand, Indians, murderers, ghost towns, and gold mines all add color to a Rio Grande trip—as will this Mexican-style breakfast.

Enchilada sauce   two 10-ounce cans
Water   ½ cup
Medium yellow onion   1, chopped
Black pepper, garlic powder, and chili powder   ½ teaspoon each
Cayenne pepper   pinch
Eggs   12
Corn tortillas   12
Cheddar cheese   ½ pound, grated
Sour cream   ½ pint

Combine enchilada sauce, water, onion, and spices in saucepan. Heat to bubbling. Gently drop eggs in without breaking yolks, a few at a time, poaching them in sauce. At the same time, warm tortillas in another pan. When eggs are done, scoop out one at a time and place on warmed tortilla. Cover with sauce and sprinkle with grated cheese. Top with sour cream.

American River Scromlet

Serves 6
Preparation time: 30 minutes

The American River is one of the most popular rivers in the country. Located in the Sierra foothills, it provides good rafting and fishing, and along its banks stands Sutter's Mill, where James Marshall's discovery of gold on January 24, 1848, touched off the famous California gold rush.

Medium yellow onion   1, chopped
Bell pepper   1, chopped
Oil   1 to 2 tablespoons
Milk powder   ¼ cup
Water   1 cup
Salt   ½ teaspoon
Black pepper and garlic powder   1 teaspoon each
Parsley flakes and tarragon   1 tablespoon each
Eggs   15
Cheddar cheese   ½ pound, grated
Sprouts   garnish

Brown onion and pepper in oil over a medium fire. Beat milk, water, spices, and herbs into eggs. Pour over browned onion and pepper. Scramble, using a spatula to keep mixture from sticking. When nearly done, scatter grated cheese over top of scromlet and heat until melted. Serve, topping with a pinch of sprouts.

Middle Fork Eggs 'n' Chilies

Serves 8
Preparation time: 30 minutes

A trip on the Middle Fork of the Salmon River in central Idaho is one of the jewels of river running. With a deep canyon, thick forests, natural hot springs, and major rapids, this trip provides the best in solitude, beauty, and challenge.

Eggs   18
Milk powder   ¼ cup
Cold water   1 cup
Black pepper and chili powder   ½ teaspoon
Garlic powder   to taste
Cayenne pepper   pinch
Diced green chilies   two 4-ounce cans, drained
Canned mushrooms   two 4-ounce cans, sliced or
     Fresh mushrooms   ¼ pound, diced
Cream cheese   8-ounce package, diced
Salsa jalapeña   8-ounce jar

Beat eggs and combine with milk powder, water, and spices. Add chilies, mushrooms, and cream cheese. Heat a well-oiled 8-inch Dutch oven. When hot, pour in egg mixture. Bake 15 minutes with 6 briquets underneath and 13 on top for a very hot oven. Serve with salsa jalapeña on the side.

Mary's Egg Foo Yung

Serves 6
Preparation time: 20 minutes

Mary has a penchant for Chinese food and suggested this recipe as an alternative to the other egg dishes.

Medium yellow onion   1, chopped
Bean sprouts   2 large handfuls
Oil   1 to 2 tablespoons
Eggs   12
Tamari or soy sauce   2 tablespoons
Black pepper   to taste

Lightly brown onion and sprouts in oil over a low fire. Beat eggs with tamari and black pepper. Pour over browned onion and sprouts, and scramble until eggs are firm. Serve immediately.

Riverbank Muffins

Serves 6
Preparation time: 10 minutes

These muffins go nicely with many of the breakfasts, or serve them alone with just a hot drink.

English muffins   6
Cream cheese   8-ounce package
Orange marmalade   10-ounce jar

Split muffins in half and toast on grill over a low fire, or toast them in a thin layer of butter in a frying pan. Spread cream cheese on muffins and top with orange marmalade.

Allagash French Toast

Serves 6
Preparation time: 20 minutes

To many the name Allagash *symbolizes freedom and the days of Thoreau. With nearly one hundred miles of connecting streams, lakes, and rivers, the Allagash is one of the most popular canoe runs in the country. Hemmed in by balsam fir and red cedar, otter and moose make their presence known while the call of the loon speaks of another time many years ago.*

Large eggs   9
Milk powder   ¼ cup
Water   1 cup
Cinnamon, nutmeg, and vanilla   1 teaspoon each
Oil   1 to 2 tablespoons
Bread   1 loaf
Plain yogurt   1 pound
Maple syrup or jam   16-ounce container

Combine eggs, milk powder, water, and spices in shallow dish, beating well. Heat an oiled frying pan or griddle over a medium fire. Dip each slice of bread into egg mixture, soaking thoroughly. Transfer to frying pan and brown on both sides. Keep first slices hot by placing in a warmed Dutch oven. Serve topped with yogurt and maple syrup or jam.

Blueberry Pancakes

Yield: twenty 5-inch cakes
Preparation time: 40 minutes

Whole wheat flour   2 cups
Milk powder   ⅓ cup
Baking powder   1 tablespoon
Baking soda   1 teaspoon
Salt   1 teaspoon
Eggs   3
Oil   3 tablespoons
Blueberries with syrup   15-ounce can
Water   1 cup
Oil   1 to 2 tablespoons
Sour cream   1 pint

Combine dry ingredients. Stir in eggs, 3 tablespoons oil, and blueberries, mixing thoroughly. Add water gradually. You may need less water than the recipe calls for, depending on the consistency of the blueberry syrup. Batter should be runny, with the consistency of warm honey. (Do not be dismayed by the purple color.) Heat a well-oiled frying pan or griddle. Test with a drop of batter—when it sizzles, the pan is hot enough to cook cakes. Drop spoonfuls of batter in pan. Brown on one side. When bubbles appear on uncooked surface, cakes are ready to flip. Brown second side. Keep first cakes hot in warm Dutch oven. Serve with sour cream topping.

Arkansas River Apple Cakes

Yield: twenty 5-inch cakes
Preparation time: 40 minutes

Near Buena Vista, Colorado, the Arkansas River cuts through narrow Brown's Canyon, offering an exciting thirteen-mile run. As the canyon opens out to high desert terrain, the river slows, and a variety of watercraft can be seen bouncing along on this easy stretch.

Whole wheat flour   2 cups
Milk powder   ⅓ cup
Baking powder   1 tablespoon
Baking soda   1 teaspoon
Salt   1 teaspoon
Cinnamon   ½ teaspoon
Eggs   3
Oil   3 tablespoons
Honey   2 tablespoons
Medium apples   2, grated
Water   1½ cups
Oil   1 to 2 tablespoons
Plain yogurt   1 pound
Applesauce   1 pound

Combine dry ingredients in a bowl. Add eggs, 3 tablespoons oil, honey, apples, and water directly to dry ingredients. Mix thoroughly. Batter should be runny, with the consistency of warm honey. Add water if necessary. Heat a well-oiled frying pan over a medium fire. Test with a drop of batter—when it sizzles the pan is hot enough to cook cakes. Drop spoonfuls of batter in pan. Brown on one side. When bubbles appear on uncooked surface, cakes are ready to flip. Brown second side. Keep first cakes hot in warm Dutch oven. Serve topped with yogurt and applesauce.

Sparkaloni's Zucchini Cakes

Yield: sixteen 4-inch cakes
Preparation time: 45 minutes

Sparky is probably the most versatile boatman I know. Equally comfortable rowing a dory or raft, he also builds beautiful custom rowing frames, plays guitar and mandolin, repairs shuttle vehicles, and cooks excellent meals. He whipped out these cakes on the spur of the moment, surprising me with a deliciously different breakfast.

Medium zucchinis   4, grated
Medium yellow onion   1, grated
Large eggs   6, beaten
Whole wheat flour   ¾ cup
Salt   ½ teaspoon
Black pepper and garlic powder   to taste
Oil   1 to 2 tablespoons
Jack cheese   ½ pound, grated

Combine zucchini, onion, eggs, flour, and spices. Resulting mixture should be wet, but not as runny as pancake batter. Heat a well-oiled frying pan or griddle over a low to medium fire. Drop large spoonfuls of mixture in pan as you do with pancake batter. Cover. Cook slowly 15 minutes on each side. When nearly done, melt cheese over top of each patty. Serve hot.

MIDDAY
MUNCHIES

The Lunch Box

When the sun is high and midday hunger pangs demand you stop, you'll be delighted to have a packed lunch box at hand. By using a special container just for this, you'll eliminate the nuisance of untying and opening a number of boxes in the middle of the day. This lunch container can be a rocket box, large ammo can, milk crate inside a waterproof bag, cooler, or one of your own making. It is best if it is somewhat rigid to prevent squishing soft foods, and the more accessible it is, the easier this meal is to prepare.

Lunch Box Checklist:
   Lunch of the day
   Tortillas/crackers/bread
   Drink of the day
   Peanut butter
   Jelly/jam/preserves
   Honey
   Gorp
   Fruit
   Salsa jalapeña
   Salt, black pepper, garlic powder
   Bowl
   Knives
   Spoons
   Can opener
   Tablecloth
   Cutting board
   Drink container

No lunch box is complete without peanut butter and jelly. As one guide put it: "It's easier to run a trip without rafts than without peanut butter." Virtually everyone likes it, and it is a wonderful filler for those still hungry after the main lunch is gone.

Many of the following lunches require a bowl for mixing ingredients; if a bowl won't fit in the lunch box, a bailer can substitute. A one- or two-gallon plastic bucket with a lid used only as a mixing bowl is perfect for groups of up to fifteen and is easily tied onto a boat. Items such as soap powder, honey, and other foodstuffs come in buckets this size, so they are easy to find.

Thirst Quenchers

A cool, refreshing beverage is welcome and necessary after rowing or paddling hard. Thirst quenchers range from beer to the beverage flowing past your boat. Avoid packing glass, since it can be dangerous both to people and to boats. Popular travel drinks include the following:

Canned juices. These are healthful, durable, and available in a large variety of flavors and sizes. Canned juices are easy to carry in a duffel bag and can be chilled by dragging them alongside the boat in a net bag.

Frozen juices. These are less expensive than canned juices, they come in a wide choice of flavors and take little space. They are not as durable as canned juices, but with a good cooling system will usually remain fresh up to a week after thawing out.

Powdered drinks. These definitely save space, but almost all contain large quantities of sugar, which tends to increase thirst rather than relieve it. Gatorade is slightly better than many of the others, as it also contains glucose, an excellent source of energy for the body.

Sun tea. This drink is easily made by putting an herbal or black tea bag in a clear container with water and setting in the sun for a few hours. After brewing to maximum strength, chill before drinking. Sun tea takes some preparation, but provides a different sort of refreshment.

Beer. Cans are easy to drag alongside the boat in a net bag. Tie it on tightly or someone else will delight in your loss. It should be noted that while beer may be refreshing on hot days, alcohol is dehydrating, which increases the risk of heat exhaustion.

Wine. This is not exactly a thirst quencher, but wine makes a nice treat for special occasions. There are a few brands that package wine-in-a-box. Inside the box is a plastic four-liter container of chablis, burgundy, or rosé, making this a safe and easy way to carry wine.

Hot drinks. These are most welcome on cold, rainy days, or any time someone takes an involuntary swim in cold water. A handy thermos of hot chocolate, sweetened coffee, or tea can literally be a lifesaver. And, of course, hot drinks can be served morning and evening in camp.

Grand Canyon Gorp

Serves 10 to 12

A trip on the Colorado River of the Grand Canyon is one of the ultimate experiences in river running. For 280 miles, from Lee's Ferry to Pierce's Ferry, the river cuts through ages of geologic time, passes by spectacular scenery, and encompasses some of the best white water in the country. The Grand demands attention and exertion. This gorp was developed there simply by combining the dried fruit we had along on a canyon trip. It is extremely tasty and provides energy after cold water and adrenalin have drained you.

	Number of Days				
	6	10	15	20	25
Figs	1	1½	2	3	3½
Dates	2	2	3	4	5
Raisins	1⅔	2	3	4	5
Dried fruit					
Banana chips	1½	2	3	4	5
Apricots	1	1½	2½	3	4
Cashews	2	3	4	6	7
Walnuts (shelled)	1¼	2	3	4	5
Carob chips	2	2½	3½	5	6
Sunflower seeds (shelled)	2	2½	3½	5	6
Unsalted peanuts	1½	2	3	4	5

(Quantities of ingredients are in pounds.)

Combine in Ziploc or freezer bags and keep handy for munching any time of day.

Hiwassee River Combo

Serves 8
Preparation time: 20 minutes

The Hiwassee River in southeastern Tennessee is an exceptionally beautiful river with cold, clear water and easy rapids. Protected as a State Scenic River, the Hiwassee's 5½-mile run is ideal for novice kayakers, canoeists, and family raft outings.

Cream cheese two 8-ounce packages
Bread or tortillas 8 servings
Avocados 3, peeled, halved, and pitted
Tomatoes 4, sliced
Medium cucumber 1, peeled and sliced
Sliced black olives two 4-ounce cans, drained
Sprouts garnish
Black pepper and garlic powder to taste
Mayonnaise and Dijon mustard to taste

Spread cream cheese on bread or tortillas. Top with remaining ingredients. Add spices and a touch of mayonnaise or mustard.

Stanislaus Guacamole

Serves 8
Preparation time: 25 minutes

The Stanislaus River in the central Sierra foothills of California was a popular white-water river for years. Clear water, a number of major rapids, beautiful side creeks, and limestone cliffs made this an enchanting place. Unfortunately, the Stanislaus has recently been covered over by the backwaters of New Melones Dam. Guacamole has long been a traditional lunch with commercial companies and private parties on Stanislaus trips.

Ripe avocados 6
Tomatoes 4, chopped
Scallions 1 bunch chopped
Chopped black olives three 4-ounce cans, drained
Lemon 1
Sour cream ½ pint
Black pepper and garlic powder to taste
Salsa jalapeña 8-ounce jar
Flour tortillas 12
Sprouts garnish

Peel, pit, and mash avocados. Add tomatoes, scallions, olives, juice and pulp of lemon, and sour cream. Add spices and salsa jalapeña to taste. Serve on flour tortillas, topped with pinch of sprouts.
Variation: There are a number of variations to Stanislaus Guacamole. The principal difference is the final ingredient. Eight ounces of softened cream cheese, mayonnaise, yogurt, or cottage cheese may be substituted for sour cream. Varying this ingredient will give five distinctly different guacamoles—try each and select a favorite.

Avocado Shrimp Tiffin

Serves 8
Preparation time: 20 minutes

This lunch is not only delicious but is truly beautiful when carefully arranged on a cutting board or plate.

Ripe avocados   10
Fresh shrimp   ½ pound, cooked or
    Canned deveined shrimp   three 4-ounce cans, drained
Celery stalks   2, finely chopped
Mayonnaise   8-ounce jar
Black pepper, chili powder, and paprika   to taste

Halve avocados, remove pits, and arrange halves hollow side up on a plate. Combine shrimp with celery, mayonnaise, and spices. Fill each avocado half with shrimp salad and serve.

Harper's Bizarre

Serves 8
Preparation time: 20 minutes

January Harper is a river guide of good skills and high energy. She created this unusual combination that has been added to the ARTA California menu. It is a rich, tasty luncheon for those who want to serve a deluxe treat.

Cream cheese   three 8-ounce packages
Fresh shrimp   ½ pound, cooked or
    Canned deveined shrimp   four 4-ounce cans, drained
Sour cream   1 pint
Scallions   1 bunch, chopped
Cucumber   1, peeled and sliced
Tomatoes   4, chopped
Flour tortillas   12 or
    Pocket bread   6

Combine first 6 ingredients in large bowl, mixing thoroughly. Serve on flour tortillas or in pocket bread.

Red Wall Cavern Spread

Serves 8
Preparation time: 15 minutes

This beautiful, vast cavern was carved in the Red Wall limestone by the Colorado River. It is one of the most popular stops on a Grand Canyon trip since it is an ideal place for lunch, photography, volleyball, Frisbee, singing, or enjoying some moments of silence.

Cream cheese   three 8-ounce packages
Medium red onion   1, minced
Chopped black olives   two 4-ounce cans, drained
Bread, crackers, or tortillas   8 servings

Mix first 3 ingredients thoroughly and serve on bread, crackers, or tortillas.

Inner Gorge Bean Dip

Serves 8
Preparation time: 10 minutes

The Inner Gorge lies at the very depths of the Grand Canyon. Here, black Vishnu schist rises sharply, the canyon narrows, and the rapids become cauldrons of towering waves. After successfully running Hance Rapid and before going into Sockdolager, we enjoyed this light lunch on a tiny river beach.

Refried beans   three 17-ounce cans
Medium red onion   1, chopped
Mayonnaise   8-ounce jar
Tortillas, crackers   8 servings
Salsa jalapeña   8-ounce jar

Combine beans, onion, and mayonnaise. Serve on tortillas or crackers. For additional zest, top with salsa jalapeña.

Marjene's Cheese Spread

Serves 8
Preparation time: 20 minutes

Marjene is a very capable boatwoman and talented musician. With her melo-dious guitar, sweet voice, and large repertoire of songs, she can entertain a group for hours. She created this spread from leftovers, adding a very delicious lunch to our menu.

Jack cheese   ¾ pound, grated
Cheddar cheese   ¾ pound, grated
Scallions   1 bunch, chopped
Celery stalks   2, chopped
Chopped black olives   4-ounce can, drained
Lemon   1
Mayonnaise   8-ounce jar
Black pepper and garlic powder   to taste
Tortillas, bread, pocket bread, crackers   8 servings
Pickle relish   8-ounce jar
Sprouts   garnish

Combine cheese, scallions, celery, olives, lemon juice and pulp, and mayon-naise. Add spices. Serve on tortillas, bread, pocket bread, or crackers. Top with pickle relish and sprouts.

Youghiogheny Egg Salad

Serves 8
Preparation time: 20 minutes

The Youghiogheny River in southwestern Pennsylvania is well known and loved throughout the East. With a long season, beautiful scenery, and numerous lively rapids, the Youghiogheny provides superb boating for inter-mediates in every style craft.

Eggs   12
Medium red onion   1, finely chopped
Celery stalks   2, chopped
Black pepper, garlic powder, and parsley flakes   to taste
Mayonnaise   8-ounce jar
Bread, tortillas, crackers   8 servings
Dill pickle chips   12-ounce jar
Sprouts   garnish

Boil eggs in shell 12 minutes at breakfast or day before a one-day trip. Return eggs to carton and place in lunch box. At lunch, peel eggs and combine with onion, celery, spices, parsley, and mayonnaise. Serve on bread, tortillas, or crackers. Top with dill pickles and sprouts.

Nantahala Fish Salad

Serves 8
Preparation time: 20 minutes

Located in southwestern North Carolina, Nantahala translates from Cherokee to "river of the noonday sun." It is aptly named, for the sun only touches the river a few hours during midday. Though the river is not difficult, a steep gradient provides almost constant white water, and wildlife abounds in the eight miles of this run through the Nantahala National Forest.

Tuna, bonito, or salmon   three 12-ounce cans, drained
Medium red onion   1, finely chopped
Medium bell pepper   1, chopped
Chopped black olives   4-ounce can, drained
Black pepper and garlic powder   to taste
Mayonnaise   8-ounce jar
Bread, tortillas, crackers   8 servings
Sprouts   garnish

Combine fish with onion, green pepper, olives, spices, and mayonnaise. Serve on bread, tortillas, or crackers. Top with sprouts.

Cheat River Cold Cuts

Serves 8
Preparation time: 15 minutes

The Cheat River in northern West Virginia plummets through a steep-walled canyon in a wild, remote area. It is a beautiful and impressive place. With continuous, complex rapids in the eleven-mile stretch, this is a run for experts only.

Assorted meats (ham, pastrami, salami, corned beef, bologna)   1 pound, sliced
Assorted cheeses (Swiss, Cheddar, Jack)   1 pound, sliced
Medium red onion   1, sliced
Tomatoes   3, sliced
Small head of iceberg lettuce   1
Dijon mustard   8-ounce jar
Mayonnaise   8-ounce jar
Rye and pumpernickel bread   1 loaf each
Dill pickles   8-ounce jar

This is a hearty lunch for hungry boaters. You might have meat and cheese sliced in advance for convenience. Spread ingredients out and make sandwiches. Serve with dill pickles on the side.

Roaring Fork Chicken Salad

Serves 8
Preparation time: 30 minutes

Beginning with a few drops of snowmelt on Independence Pass, the Roaring Fork River rushes headlong down the west slope of the Rockies of central Colorado. There is a popular and easy one-day float shortly before it joins the Colorado River.

Chicken four 6¾-ounce cans, chopped
Water chestnuts 8-ounce can, drained and chopped
Medium red onion 1, chopped
Celery stalks 2, chopped
Plain yogurt 1 pound
Black pepper and garlic powder ½ teaspoon each
Thyme and tarragon 1 teaspoon each
Paprika ¼ teaspoon
Tortillas, bread, pocket bread, crackers 8 servings

Put chicken in bowl and stir in remaining ingredients, spices, and herbs.
Serve on tortillas, bread, pocket bread, or crackers.

Matkatamiba Lunch

Serves 10
Preparation time: 10 minutes

*If any place in the Grand Canyon is enchanted, it is Matkatamiba. After you
enter Matkatamiba through a narrow chasm, it suddenly opens up to a
natural amphitheater complete with a stage perfect for a Shakespearean play
or symphony orchestra. This lunch is a reminder of a special afternoon in this
beautiful place.*

Sardines 3¾-ounce can, drained
Hard salami 13-ounce package, sliced
Cheddar, Jack, and Swiss cheese 1 pound total, sliced
Cream cheese 8-ounce package
Medium red onion 1, sliced
Medium cucumber 1, peeled and sliced
Tomatoes 3, sliced
Sliced black olives two 4-ounce cans, drained
Dill pickles 8-ounce jar
Mayonnaise 8-ounce jar
Mustard 8-ounce jar
Bread, tortillas, crackers 10 servings

Ingredients may be combined in a variety of ways and put on bread, tortillas,
or crackers. Enjoy!
Note: This is a handy lunch for an extended trip, since most of the ingredients keep a long time.

Little Colorado Hummus

Serves 8
Preparation time: 15 minutes

The confluence of the Colorado and Little Colorado rivers marks the beginning of The Great Unknown *as described by Major John Wesley Powell on his pioneer voyage through the Grand Canyon. With warm water and mud baths available, it is a popular and relaxing place to stop.*

Garbanzo beans   three 15-ounce cans, drained
Medium red onion   1, minced
Medium bell pepper   1, chopped
Lemon juice and pulp   of 1 lemon
Mayonnaise   8-ounce jar
Tahini   4 tablespoons
Garlic powder   1 teaspoon
Cumin and black pepper   ½ teaspoon each
Tortillas, pocket bread, crackers   8 servings

Drain and mash garbanzo beans. Stir in remaining ingredients, mixing thoroughly. Serve on tortillas, pocket bread, or crackers.

River Cheesecake

While working as a commercial guide in California, I discovered this simple luncheon dessert. The guides would make up a "river cheesecake" and show it to the passengers, who invariably turned up their noses. Once urged to try it (and succumbing), however, they had a completely different and delighted reaction.

Oatmeal cookies
Cream cheese
Jam or preserves

Spread cream cheese on cookie for plain "cheesecake." Add jam or preserves for flavored "cheesecake."

HORS D'OEUVRES AND A SALAD BAR

Hors d'Oeuvres

Serves 8 to 10
Preparation time: 10 to 15 minutes

Simple hors d'oeuvres can complement a gourmet meal, make an impression on your fellow travelers, and help take the edge off their appetite (and yours) while you are preparing dinner.

Sour Cream Dip

Sour cream   1 pint
Onion soup mix   1 envelope
Wheat Thins   1 box

Mix sour cream and onion soup mix together. Serve with crackers.

Mexican Dip

Salsa jalapeña   8-ounce jar
Tortilla chips   two 7-ounce bags

Put salsa in a bowl and serve with chips.

Horseradish Dip

Horseradish sauce   ¼ cup
Black pepper, paprika, Tabasco, and parsley flakes   to taste
Sour cream   ½ pint
Carrots   6
Celery   1 bunch

Mix horseradish sauce, black pepper, paprika, and Tabasco with sour cream. Sprinkle with parsley. Cut carrots in half crosswise, then slice lengthwise to make 2- to 3-inch spears. Cut celery into 3-inch stalks. Serve with dip.

Spicy Dip

Sour cream ½ pint
Mayonnaise 2 tablespoons
Tamari or soy sauce 1 tablespoon
Scallions 1 bunch, finely chopped
Dijon mustard 1 tablespoon
Curry powder, ginger, paprika, and parsley flakes to taste
Wheat Thins 1 box

Combine all ingredients in a bowl, mixing thoroughly. Serve with crackers.

Cheese Board

Cheddar cheese ¼ pound
Monterey Jack cheese ¼ pound
Brie or Camembert ¼ pound
Gouda ¼ pound
Rye Krisp or Ak-Mak crackers 1 box

Arrange cheeses on a cutting board alongside a sharp knife.
Serve with crackers.
Note: This is a perfect time to bring out that wine you've been saving.

Salad Dressings

Ready-made dressings are available, many in plastic bottles, but if you wish to make your own, the following will add variety to your salads.

Tangy Dressing

Mayonnaise 8-ounce jar
Wine vinegar 3 tablespoons
Lemon juice and pulp of 1 lemon
Black pepper, garlic powder, dry mustard, cumin, turmeric, and cayenne pepper to taste

Herbal Dressing

Apple juice ½ cup
Cider vinegar ½ cup
Lemon juice and pulp of 1 lemon
Black pepper, onion powder, garlic powder, dry mustard, paprika, oregano, thyme, and rosemary to taste

Yogurt Dressing

Plain yogurt   ½ pound
Wine vinegar   2 tablespoons
Dill seed, black pepper, onion powder, garlic powder, and parsley flakes
    to taste

Creamy Tamari Dressing

Sour cream   ½ pint
Mayonnaise   ¼ cup
Tamari or soy sauce   ¼ cup
Black pepper and garlic powder   to taste

These four dressings will complement any of the following salads. In each case, combine the ingredients in a bowl or in a 16-ounce jar with a lid and mix thoroughly. If time allows, make the dressing an hour ahead of serving to give the flavors a chance to blend.

Camp-Grown Sprouts

Growing sprouts is really quite simple, and on long river trips, it will enable you to add a fresh, green touch to sandwiches, salads, and other meals.

Jars, trays, and sacks make excellent sprouting containers, with growing time and requirements the same for each. Jars require cheesecloth or mosquito netting as a cover and rubber bands to hold the cloth on the jar. Plastic jars are available from restaurants and are preferable to glass since they are unbreakable. Gallon jars can be carried three to a large ammo box or four to a milk crate. For very small trips with only a few people, quart containers are adequate. Trays may be purchased from health food stores and could be stacked in a milk crate. Sacks can be made out of mosquito netting and should have a tight drawstring to prevent seeds from escaping out the top if the sack becomes inverted. Sacks are easily carried by tying them to the boat. In order to have fresh sprouts at all times, begin a new crop of seeds one and two days after the first batch is started.

Alfalfa Sprouts

Yield: 2 to 3 cups

Alfalfa seeds   2 tablespoons
Water   2 cups

See description of sprouting containers in preceding paragraph. Cover bottom of desired container with alfalfa seeds. Fill jar with water or place trays and sacks in water overnight. The following morning, pour water out of jar or take tray and sacks out of water. Thereafter, rinse twice daily by pouring water into jar or through tray, or by dipping sacks in water. Keep seeds away from intense sunlight until they are fully matured sprouts. Then place them in the sun for a few hours to develop the chlorophyll and a nice green color.
Note: Alfalfa seeds take 3 to 5 days to fully sprout in warm weather. When I grew alfalfa sprouts on a cold weather trip, they took over a week to mature.

Cucumber Salad

Serves 8

Cucumbers   4 large
Red onion   1 medium
Radishes   1 bunch
Mandarin orange sections   two 11-ounce cans

Thinly slice cucumbers, onion, and radishes. Place in bowl. Drain juice from mandarin orange sections and add segments to salad. Serve with Italian dressing.

Corn Salad

Serves 8

Corn kernels   three 17-ounce cans
Red onion   1 medium
Pimentos   two 4-ounce jars

Thinly slice red onion and drain liquid from corn kernels. Combine in bowl with pimentos and serve with Italian dressing.

Ferg's Zephyr Salad

Preparation time: 40 minutes

This is the traditional dinner salad of Bob Ferguson's Zephyr River Expeditions of California, and is unanimously acclaimed by guides and passengers.

	Number of People			
	4	**7**	**10**	**15**
Lettuce: Red leaf	1	1	1	1
Romaine		1	1	1
Iceberg			1	1
Red cabbage		1 small	1 small	1 medium
Spinach (bunch)			1	1
Red onions	1 small	1 medium	1 medium	1 large
Carrots	2	4	5	6
Cucumbers	1 small	1 small	1 medium	1 medium
Tomatoes	2	4	6	8
Radishes (bunch)	1	1	1	1
Parsley (bunch)	1	1	1	1
Mushrooms (pounds)	½	½	¾	1
Bottled artichoke hearts	4 ounces	4 ounces	8 ounces	12 ounces
Canned kidney beans	8 ounces	15 ounces	15 ounces	30 ounces
Canned garbanzo beans	8 ounces	15 ounces	15 ounces	30 ounces
Shrimp (pounds)	⅓	½	¾	1
Sprouts	garnish			

Chop ingredients, combine in a large bowl, and toss. Serve salad dressing on side so leftovers may be saved.

Selway Greek Salad

Serves 8
Preparation time: 30 minutes

Dip your cup into the crystal clear water, feast your eyes on the exquisite scenery, drink in the fresh, pure air, and carefully scout the challenging rapids, for this is the Selway tumbling through the largest wilderness area in the United States. Put-in for a Selway trip is at Paradise—and it gets better from there!

Medium head of iceberg lettuce 1
Tomatoes 5
Medium cucumber 1, peeled
Avocado 1, peeled
Bell pepper 1
Medium red onion 1
Feta cheese ½ pound, cubed
Pitted black olives 6-ounce can, drained
Pitted green olives 6-ounce can, drained

Cut vegetables into large pieces. Toss in a bowl with cheese and olives. Add desired dressing just before serving.

Chef's Salad

Serves 8
Preparation time: 30 minutes

Eggs 8
Head of romaine lettuce 1, shredded
Ham ¾ pound, thinly sliced
Roast beef ¾ pound, thinly sliced
Swiss cheese ½ pound, cubed
Cheddar cheese ½ pound, cubed
Scallions 1 bunch, chopped
Tomatoes 3, chopped
Cucumber 1, peeled and sliced
Artichoke hearts two 6-ounce jars, drained

Boil eggs 12 minutes in saucepan, then put them in cold water to cool. Place lettuce in bottom of bowl. Shell eggs and slice crosswise. Arrange meat, cheese, eggs, and vegetables on top of lettuce. Serve with desired dressing.
Note: This salad is a meal in itself and ideal for a hot weather dinner.

Kings River Spinach Salad

Serves 6
Preparation time: 30 minutes

The Kings River drops out of Kings Canyon high in the Sierra of California. Along its course, the Kings provides some of California's largest white water. Wild flowers, oak, and pine cover the steep foothills and a side creek complete with natural slides and whirlpool baths offers a contrast to the white water.

Eggs   6
Spinach leaves   1 large bunch
Mushrooms   ½ pound, chopped
Scallions   1 bunch, chopped

Boil eggs 12 minutes in saucepan. Put eggs in cold water to cool. Wash spinach in clear water and tear leaves into small pieces. Shell eggs and slice crosswise. Combine all ingredients in bowl and serve with desired dressing.
Note: Because spinach and mushrooms do not keep well, this salad is best served the first day of a trip.

Potato Salad

Serves 8
Preparation time: 30 minutes

Medium potatoes   8
Eggs   4
Celery stalks   3, chopped
Sliced black olives   two 4-ounce cans, drained
Dill pickles   6-ounce jar, diced
Mayonnaise   8-ounce jar
Wine vinegar   2 tablespoons
Dijon mustard   1 tablespoon
Salt, black pepper, and parsley flakes   to taste

Wash potatoes in clear water and boil whole for 1 hour the morning before this salad is planned. At the same time, boil eggs 12 minutes. Place cooked potatoes and hard-cooked eggs in a cool box during the day. At dinner, cut potatoes in small pieces and combine in a bowl with remaining ingredients.

Dolores River Tabouleh

Serves 6
Preparation time: 1½ hours

The Dolores River begins in the mountains of southwestern Colorado and continues on through sandstone canyons. Two popular canyon runs provide boaters with weekend and week-long trips of beautiful desert scenery. Most of the rapids are moderate except for the difficult Snaggletooth.

Water   3 cups
Salt   ½ teaspoon
Bulgur wheat   2 cups uncooked
Tomatoes   2, chopped
Medium red onion   1, chopped
Fresh mint   2 tablespoons or
    Dried mint   1 teaspoon
Medium lemons, juice and pulp   2
Salad oil   ½ cup
Parsley flakes, garlic powder, and black pepper   1 tablespoon each

Bring salted water to a boil. Add bulgur slowly and keep boiling for a few minutes. Cover. Remove pot from heat and set aside for 1 hour. Drain off excess water and chill grain by placing bottom of pot in cold water or putting in a cooler for 15 minutes. Stir in remaining ingredients. Serve as a main course on a hot summer night.

Hudson River Macaroni Salad

Serves 8
Preparation time: 30 minutes

Between its source at Lake Tear of the Clouds and Luzerne, the Hudson River has New York's finest white water. Whether raging through the natural beauty of the Hudson Gorge or sliding placidly past mountains and meadows, the Upper Hudson offers a delightful journey through the Adirondack wilderness.

Water   4 cups
Oil   1 tablespoon
Elbow macaroni   1 pound
Medium red onion   1, chopped
Celery   1 bunch, chopped
Mayonnaise   8-ounce jar
Wine vinegar   2 tablespoons
Paprika, black pepper, and celery seed   to taste
French dressing   8-ounce bottle

Bring water and oil to a boil in a large saucepan. Add macaroni and cook until tender. (This is best done well ahead of time so cooked macaroni may be chilled in a cooler.) When ready to serve, mix macaroni with remaining ingredients. Use French dressing as garnish.

Missouri River Salad

Serves 6 to 8
Preparation time: 20 minutes

Silently dip your paddle into the fast, narrow upper Missouri and glide along the route of Lewis and Clark. Natural buttresses of white rock reflect in the river as you pass sites that allude to times when Indians, explorers, and homesteaders frequented the shores.

Medium head of green cabbage   1, shredded
Medium red apples   4, diced
Sunflower seeds   1 cup shelled
Raisins   1 cup

Combine all ingredients in a bowl. Select a dressing and serve.
Note: This is a durable salad, ideal for long trips.

Tamarisk Hilton Salad

Serves 6
Preparation time: 20 minutes

Tamarisk trees line the beaches of many desert river canyons. With a feathery softness, they bend in the lightest breeze and provide shade during the heat of the day. This salad was created at one such camp.

Medium red apples   5, diced
Pineapple chunks   8-ounce can, drained
Medium carrots   4, grated
Celery   1 bunch, chopped
Walnuts   1 cup chopped
Raisins   1 cup
Cinnamon and nutmeg   to taste

Combine all ingredients in a bowl. Serve with desired dressing.

Gauley Bean Salad

Serves 8
Preparation time: 20 minutes

The Gauley, located in central West Virginia, stands out as the finest big white-water run in the East. A twenty-four-mile section from Summersville Dam to Swiss rages through a steep-walled canyon. Most of the numerous rapids here are for experts only. On this river, even commercial passengers must have prior experience.

Kidney beans   15-ounce can
Pinto beans   15-ounce can
Garbanzo beans   15-ounce can
Green beans   15-ounce can
Asparagus tips   15-ounce can
Artichoke hearts   6-ounce jar
Medium red onion   1, chopped
Salad oil   ½ cup
Wine vinegar   3 tablespoons
Garlic powder and black pepper   to taste

Drain liquid off beans, asparagus tips, and artichoke hearts. Combine with onion, oil, vinegar, and spices in a large bowl. Serve.

Westwater Carrot Salad

Serves 6
Preparation time: 20 minutes

Westwater Canyon in eastern Utah begins in the open desert. Then, suddenly, sheer sandstone and schist walls compress the Colorado River into a narrow, raging turmoil. It is an exhilarating run with awesome scenery and lovely calm stretches before and after the rapids.

Medium carrots   10, grated
Raisins   2 cups
Sunflower seeds   1 cup shelled
Cinnamon and nutmeg   to taste

Combine ingredients with spices in bowl. Serve with selected dressing.

BREADS,
SOUPS, AND
SIDE DISHES

Whole Wheat Bread

Yield: 2 loaves
Preparation time: 3 to 4 hours

Baking bread involves a time commitment which may be unsuitable for your river trip. If you do have the time and energy, however, try it. I remember one trip when I elected to bake bread while everyone else was hiking. When my friends returned to the freshly baked loaves they were ecstatic, and I felt good too. In fact, all we had for dinner that night was bread and butter with hot tea. It was a true feast.

Water 2¾ cups
Milk powder ½ cup
Salt 2 teaspoons
Butter or margarine 1 tablespoon or
    Oil 2 tablespoons
Honey ⅓ cup
Active dry yeast 2 tablespoons
Whole wheat flour 6 cups

Combine water, milk powder, salt, butter, and honey. It may be necessary to liquefy butter and honey in order to obtain a smooth mixture. This is easily done by heating the water first in a separate pot and then combining the ingredients. Select a bowl or pan large enough to hold liquid plus flour and still allow room for the dough to rise.

Bring mixture to a temperature of 90 to 100 degrees Fahrenheit, by either heating additionally or allowing mixture to cool. If a thermometer is not available, use your finger. Since this temperature range is close to your body temperature, the liquid will feel neither hot nor cold. When liquid has reached correct temperature, add yeast, stirring in well. Set in a warm place. On a sunny day, a black pot with a black cover placed in the sun will draw enough solar heat to keep the dough warm. Or, put pot or bowl next to (not on) fire. When yeast begins to froth, it is time to add flour. Have the following utensils handy: a large spoon to take flour out of its container, a wooden spoon for the first stages of mixing the flour with the liquid, a butter knife to scrape the dough off your hands, and a washbowl with clean water for your hands.

Add flour to liquid a few spoonfuls at a time, blending thoroughly. If your flour is fairly coarse, sift it through a strainer to help the dough rise more quickly. Begin stirring flour into liquid with the wooden spoon, and as mixture thickens, use your hands. Continue adding flour until dough is slightly moist but no longer sticks to your hands. Shape into a mound, cover to prevent dough from drying out, and set in a warm spot. Dough should rise to double its size, so if a pot lid will prevent it from rising, cover with a dark cloth. (Dark colors absorb more solar heat than light colors do.)

While dough is rising, heat a well-oiled 10-inch Dutch oven.

After it rises sufficiently, which should take 20 to 30 minutes, place dough on a floured cutting board. Knead, turning and punching dough down, for about 10 minutes. Divide dough in half and form 2 oblong loaves. Place loaves across from each other in Dutch oven. As they rise, they will come together but are easily pulled apart after they are baked. Once again, place in a warm spot and allow dough to rise until it is an inch from top of the Dutch oven. This rising may take anywhere from ½ hour to 1 hour, or occasionally longer.

While dough is rising, start briquets. Timing is very important here. If dough appears to be rising quickly, begin briquets when it is halfway to top of pan. With slow-rising dough, wait until it has risen almost completely. Remember, briquets take 10 to 15 minutes to heat.

When dough has risen and briquets are gray, bake for 1¼ hours using 6 briquets underneath and 11 on top. The nose test is invaluable here and is virtually fail-proof. If you are in doubt, however, confirm by sticking a knife in the center of 1 loaf. If it comes out clean, your bread is done.

Chinese Camp Garlic Bread

Serves 8
Preparation time: 30 minutes

Chinese Camp is a large, beautiful camp along the Stanislaus River. I've spent many nights at this special place, and the name always brings back vivid memories of good times with wonderful people. This bread was served regularly on our overnight stops at Chinese Camp and never failed to make a big hit with everyone.

Butter   ¼ pound
Garlic powder   2 teaspoons
French bread   1 loaf
Paprika   1 teaspoon

Melt butter with garlic powder in a small pan at edge of fire. Slice loaf lengthwise and spread mixture over inside of both halves. Sprinkle lightly with paprika. Put halves together and slice crosswise. Wrap completely in foil. Place at edge of fire and heat slowly on both sides. In the event you do not have a fire, melt butter and garlic in large frying pan. Toast slices of bread in pan on stove.

New River Corn Bread

Yield: 8-inch round loaf
Preparation time: 1 hour

Flowing through the Allegheny mountains of West Virginia the New River is known as the Grand Canyon of the East. With high-volume water and a constricted riverbed, some classic and impressive rapids have been formed offering an exhilarating river adventure.

Cornmeal   1½ cups
Whole wheat flour   ½ cup
Milk powder   ¼ cup
Baking powder   2 teaspoons
Baking soda   1 teaspoon
Eggs   2
Oil   2 tablespoons
Honey   ¼ cup
Water   ½ cup
Chopped green chilies   two 4-ounce cans
Cheddar cheese   ¼ pound, grated

Combine cornmeal, flour, milk powder, baking powder, and baking soda in bowl. Add eggs, oil, honey, and water directly to dry ingredients. Heat a well-oiled 8-inch Dutch oven. Pour half the mixture into pan, spread chilies and cheese on top. Pour in remaining mixture and bake 45 minutes with 4 briquets underneath and 9 on top for a medium oven.

Susquehanna Biscuits

Yield: eighteen 2½-inch biscuits
Preparation time: 30 minutes

Between its West Branch, North Branch, and Main Stem, the Susquehanna River in Pennsylvania provides hundreds of miles of good canoeing. Much of this river still retains its wilderness character as it flows through rugged, hilly countryside. It's ideal for a scenic spring river trip.

Milk powder   ¼ cup
Water   ⅔ cup
Bisquick   2 cups
Oil   1 to 2 tablespoons
Butter   1 tablespoon, melted

Mix milk powder with water and add to Bisquick. If dough is sticky, gradually add more Bisquick until it feels dry to the touch. Turn dough out onto a well-floured cutting board and knead for about 30 seconds. Let dough stand about 5 minutes so biscuits will rise better while cooking. Press out flat with the palm of your hand to about ¼-inch thickness. Heat a well-oiled frying pan or griddle over medium heat. Cut dough into eighteen 2½-inch biscuits. Brush each biscuit with melted butter or oil and place in pan. Cover. Cook about 5 minutes on each side. Cook biscuits slowly or they will burn on the outside and remain uncooked inside. Serve hot with butter.

Shortcutt's Specialty

Serves 8
Preparation time: 20 mintues

Shortcutt is one hell of a dynamic woman. Whether she is kayaking, playing her fiddle or guitar, or whipping out a meal, she does it well, with zest and vitality. This unusual and delicious recipe is a good example and makes a hit every time.

Mayonnaise   ½ cup
Parmesan cheese   ½ cup grated
Parsley flakes   ½ cup
Scallions   ¼ cup chopped
Horseradish sauce   1 tablespoon
Seasoned salt   1 tablespoon
French bread   1 loaf
Jack cheese   ¼ pound, grated

Combine mayonnaise, Parmesan cheese, parsley, scallions, horseradish sauce, and seasoned salt, mixing thoroughly. Slice bread in half lengthwise. Spread mixture over each half. Top with grated cheese. Cut bread in smaller pieces and put in heated 10-inch Dutch oven. Bake 3 to 10 minutes with 7 briquets underneath and 15 on top for a very hot oven. Or, put bread in a large frying pan or griddle, cover, and heat 3 to 10 minutes. Bread should be served hot after the cheese has melted.

Kate's Spoon Bread

Serves 8
Preparation time: 1 hour

After Kate and I met on a Grand Canyon trip, we became friends and began to plan other trips together. During one of our visits she made this excellent bread, and I quickly added it to my list of outstanding recipes.

Flour   ½ cup
Cornmeal   1½ cups
Sugar   2 tablespoons
Salt   2 teaspoons
Baking powder   2 teaspoons
Baking soda   1 teaspoon
Eggs   2
Buttermilk   1¾ cups
Corn kernels   one 17-ounce can, drained

Stir dry ingredients together. Add eggs, corn, and 1¼ cups buttermilk. Pour into a well-oiled 10-inch Dutch oven. Pour ½ cup buttermilk over the top. Bake 45 minutes with 6 briquets underneath and 13 on top for a medium oven.

Drifter's Onion Soup

Serves 6
Preparation time: 30 minutes

A Grand Canyon boatman of many talents, Drifter created this recipe which was quickly adopted by Arizona Raft Adventures for their menu.

Medium yellow onions   4, coarsely chopped
Onion soup mix   2 envelopes
Black pepper, garlic powder, and dry mustard   1 teaspoon each
Basil and thyme   1 tablespoon
Water   6 cups
English muffins   6
Parmesan cheese   1 pound, grated

Place onions, soup mix, spices, and herbs in saucepan with water. Bring to a boil and simmer 10 minutes. Remove from fire. Break up English muffins and drop pieces into soup. Serve, topping with Parmesan cheese.

Cabbage Onion Soup

Serves 6
Preparation time: 45 minutes

Large head of red cabbage   1, shredded
Medium yellow onions   3, sliced
Garlic cloves   5, peeled and minced
Tamari or soy sauce   ½ cup
Black pepper, salt, dill seed, basil, and celery seed   ½ teaspoon each or
    to taste
Jack cheese   ½ pound, grated

Place cabbage, onions, and garlic in large pot with enough water to cover
them. Cover pot and bring to a boil. Lower heat and cook at a high simmer
15 minutes. Add tamari and herbs, simmering another 10 minutes. Serve,
topping with grated cheese.

Corn Chowder

Serves 4
Preparation time: 40 minutes

Margarine   1 tablespoon
Yellow onion   1 medium, chopped
Celery   1 stalk, chopped
Bell pepper   1 very small, chopped
Flour   1 tablespoon
Paprika   ½ teaspoon
Chicken broth   1 cup
Whole kernel corn   one 17-ounce can
Nonfat dry milk   ¼ cup
Water   1 cup
Lemon juice   1½ teaspoons
Black pepper   ⅛ teaspoon

Melt margarine in a 10-inch Dutch oven over medium heat. Add onion,
celery, and bell pepper, and cook until soft, about 5 minutes. Stir in flour and
paprika, and continue to cook. Add chicken broth, and turn up heat so mixture comes to a boil. Add corn, cover, and cook about 5 minutes. Mix dry
milk with water, and add to vegetables. Reduce heat, and stir in lemon juice
and black pepper. (Do not allow soup to boil or it will curdle.) Serve.

Hermit Creek Potato Soup

Serves 8
Preparation time: 1¼ hours

Hermit Rapid, with its towering haystacks, surges by at the confluence of Hermit Creek and the Colorado River. Hidden among tamarisk trees and large boulders is a small camp where this soup was created. Camping here also gave us the opportunity to watch other parties run Hermit and to antici- pate the exhilaration of running it ourselves the following morning.

Medium potatoes   12, diced
Medium carrots   5, chopped
Medium yellow onions   2, chopped
Milk powder   ½ cup
**Black pepper, garlic powder, dill seed, celery seed, parsley flakes,
     oregano, and tarragon**   to taste

Wash potatoes and carrots in clear water. Combine vegetables in pot with ample water to cover. Cover pot and bring to a boil. Cook at a high simmer 45 minutes. Stir in milk powder, spices, and herbs. Simmer an additional 10 minutes. Serve.
Note: Save leftovers for the following day's lunch. Mix ½ cup milk powder with 1 cup of cold water and add it to the soup to make an excellent vichyssoise.

Dr. Rouzer's Gazpacho

Serves 6
Preparation time: 40 minutes

Steve Rouzer, M.D., does as much canyon hiking and rafting as his busy schedule allows. This soup was served on a remarkable San Juan trip that he put together, and brings back memories of a costume party, charades by flashlight, and a very congenial group of people.

Tomatoes   5
Small cucumber   1, peeled
Scallions   1 bunch
Bell pepper   1
Garlic clove   1, peeled
Tomato juice   1 pint
Olive oil   ¼ cup

Wine vinegar ¼ cup
Water ¼ cup
**Black pepper, cayenne pepper, dill seed, oregano, celery seed, and
parsley flakes** to taste

Chop tomatoes, cucumber, scallions, bell pepper, and garlic into small pieces. Combine in a large bowl. Pour in tomato juice. Combine olive oil, vinegar, water, spices, and herbs in a separate bowl. Pour over vegetables, mixing thoroughly. Serve.

Swiss Beans

Serves 8
Preparation time: 20 minutes

This is an example of turning a canned vegetable into a special side dish.

French-style green beans three 15-ounce cans, drained or
1 pound fresh, trimmed
Medium yellow onion 1, chopped
Swiss cheese ½ pound, grated
Butter or margarine 2 tablespoons
Sour cream ½ cup
Black pepper, garlic powder, and paprika ¼ teaspoon each

Heat beans and onion in a saucepan 10 minutes over medium fire. Drain off water and stir in cheese, butter, sour cream, and spices.

Cauliflower and Cheese

Serves 8
Preparation time: 25 minutes

Medium cauliflowers 2
Sharp Cheddar cheese ½ pound, grated
Parsley flakes, tarragon, and basil 1 tablespoon each

Break cauliflower into flowerets and wash in clear water. Steam or boil in small amount of water about 15 minutes. Remove from heat and drain. Stir in cheese and herbs. Cover a few minutes to allow cheese to melt. Serve hot.

Patch's Irish Potatoes

Serves 8
Preparation time: 45 minutes

As my friends know, I love potatoes and often have them as a main course. Potatoes are versatile, delicious, healthful, and filling. When I added these spices to liven up plain boiled potatoes, even I was amazed at how much people enjoyed them.

Medium potatoes   8 to 10
Butter or margarine   ½ cup
Black pepper, garlic powder, parsley flakes, oregano, tarragon, dill seed, and celery seed   ½ teaspoon each

Wash potatoes in clear water and cut in small pieces. Put in a saucepan, cover with water, and boil about 30 minutes until tender. Drain off water. Stir in butter, spices, and herbs.

Sweet and Sour Cabbage

Serves 8
Preparation time: 30 minutes

Medium yellow onion   1, coarsely chopped
Oil   2 tablespoons
Medium apple   1, grated
Medium green cabbage   1, shredded
Water   ¼ cup
Honey   2 tablespoons
Whole wheat flour   2 tablespoons
Wine vinegar   2 tablespoons
Salt   1 teaspoon
Water   ½ cup

Sauté onion in oil until soft. Add apple, cabbage, and ¼ cup water to onion. Cook 5 minutes. Heat honey until it liquefies and combine with flour, vinegar, salt, and ½ cup water, mixing well. Stir mixture into cabbage and cook over medium heat another 5 to 10 minutes. Serve.

Artichokes

Serves 4
Preparation time: 50 minutes

Medium to large artichokes 4

Cut stem off artichokes close to leaves and wash in clear water. Steam or boil 30 to 50 minutes. Test by sticking a fork into base of artichoke where stem meets leaves. When tender it is ready to serve. Use Tangy Dressing (see Index), plain mayonnaise, or melted butter as a dip for leaves.

Note: Artichokes can be used as a side dish before a main course or served with a salad for a light meal.

Honeyed Carrots

Serves 8
Preparation time: 30 minutes

Medium carrots 15, cut in small chunks
Butter or margarine ½ cup
Honey ¼ cup
Rosemary, thyme, and basil ¼ teaspoon each

Steam or boil carrots, covered, in a small amount of water until tender. Melt butter and honey together. When liquefied, stir in herbs. Pour over cooked carrots.

Broccoli and Lemon Butter

Serves 8
Preparation time: 25 minutes

Broccoli 3 pounds, trimmed
Butter ½ cup
Lemon 1
Garlic powder and black pepper ½ teaspoon each
Oregano 1 teaspoon

Cut broccoli into ¼-inch slices. Break flowerets apart and cut leaves off stem. (Do not throw leaves away, since they contain most of the nutritives.) Steam or boil for 15 minutes. While broccoli is cooking, melt butter and scrub lemon thoroughly in clear water. Squeeze lemon juice and pulp into butter. Grate half the lemon peel and add to butter. Add spices and oregano, blending thoroughly, and pour over cooked broccoli.

Applesauce Cayenne

Serves 6
Preparation time: 5 minutes

Applesauce   three 16-ounce cans
Plain yogurt   1 pound
Cayenne pepper   pinch

Combine applesauce and yogurt. Add cayenne to taste. Serve.

VEGIE
DELIGHTS

Beans and rice are so often an integral part of vegetarian cooking that I have provided the following table on cooking dried legumes and a recipe for "Basic Brown Rice." These will be referred to in the ingredient lists for many of the recipes in this chapter.

Couscous

Serves 4
Preparation time: 10 minutes

Couscous is made from coarsely ground durum wheat that has been pre-cooked. A traditional dish of the North African countries of Morocco, Algeria, and Tunisia, it is an alternative to rice or pasta and can be found in most large grocery stores or health food stores.

Water   2½ cups
Margarine   4 tablespoons
Couscous   2 cups

Bring water and margarine to boil. Add couscous. Stir. Remove from heat and allow to stand 5 minutes. Stir to fluff up. Serve.

Pancho's Rice

Serves 8
Preparation time: 30 minutes

Oil   ¼ cup
Quick white or brown rice   3 cups
Medium yellow onion   1, chopped
Celery   2 large stalks, chopped
Medium bell pepper   1, chopped
Chili powder, cumin, oregano   to taste
Canned whole tomatoes   one 24-ounce can
Water   2⅔ cups

Heat oil in deep pan. Fry rice and onion, stirring constantly, 3 to 5 minutes. Add celery, bell pepper, and spices; cook another 5 minutes. Add tomatoes with juice and water. Cook 10 minutes. Serve.

Basic Brown Rice

Serves 8
Preparation time: 1 hour

Brown rice 4 cups uncooked
Water 8 cups
Salt ½ teaspoon or
  Tamari or soy sauce 2 tablespoons

Wash rice in plain cold water. Set to one side. Put salt in water and bring to boil. Add rice and simmer covered 50 to 60 minutes. Do not stir rice while cooking. Serve cooked rice with many of the following recipes.

Robb's Peanut Stew

Serves 8
Preparation time: 1 hour

Boatman and photographer Robb Moss discovered this unusual dish in North Africa. For authenticity, it should be very spicy.

Carrots 5, chopped
Small red cabbage 1, shredded
Corn 15-ounce can, drained
Green beans 15-ounce can, drained
Milk powder ½ cup
Water 2 cups
Peanut butter 1 cup
Raw cashews 1 cup chopped
Cayenne pepper and garlic powder to taste
Basic Brown Rice (see Index) 8 cups

Combine carrots, cabbage, corn, green beans, milk powder, and water in saucepan. Simmer 15 minutes. Do not overcook vegetables—they should be crunchy. Stir in peanut butter, cashews, and spices. Heat 10 minutes. Serve over rice.

Owyhee Stir-Fry

Preparation time: 1 hour

The Owyhee River in southeastern Oregon was named after a group of Hawaiian fur trappers who disappeared along its course in the early 1800s. Isolated and remote, the Owyhee affords the boater a beautiful desert canyon trip.

	Number of People			
	5	**8**	**10**	**15**
Onions	1 small	1 medium	1 large	2 medium
Carrots	1 large	2 medium	2 large	3 large
Broccoli (pounds)	½	¾	1	1½
Cauliflower	1 small	1 small	1 medium	1 medium
Red cabbage	1 small	1 small	1 medium	1 medium
Yellow squash	1 small	1 medium	2 small	2 medium
Zucchini	1 small	1 medium	2 small	2 medium
Green beans (pounds)	¼	½	¾	1
Mushrooms (pounds)	¼	⅓	½	¾
Raw cashews (pounds)	¼	⅓	½	¾
Jack cheese (pounds)	1	1½	2	2½
Oil				

Tamari or soy sauce, black pepper, and garlic powder   to taste

Chop vegetables in large pieces. Grate cheese. Heat oil in frying pan or griddle. Add vegetables beginning with onions, carrots, broccoli, cauliflower, and cabbage. Cook 5 minutes, stirring frequently. Add remaining vegetables and cashews. Stir in tamari, black pepper, and garlic powder. Cover. Cook over low heat 5 minutes so vegetables will absorb spices. Top with grated cheese.

Note: Vegetables may be varied according to taste and availability. And, remember, leftovers can always be saved and reheated.

Orange Sweet Potato Casserole

Serves 6
Preparation time: 35 minutes

Sweet potatoes (yams) two 29-ounce cans
Margarine ¼ cup, melted
Brown sugar ¼ cup
Mandarin oranges two 11-ounce cans
Pecans ½ cup, chopped

Combine sweet potatoes with margarine, brown sugar, and one can of mandarin oranges. Put mixture in a well-seasoned 8-inch Dutch oven. Top with second can of mandarin oranges and chopped pecans. Bake 30 minutes with 4 briquets underneath and 9 on top for a medium oven. Serve.

Yampa Bean Casserole

Serves 8
Preparation time: 1 hour

The Yampa is the last free-flowing river in the entire Colorado River system. With wild white water in Cross Mountain Canyon and a beautiful, easier run through the sandstone cliffs in Dinosaur National Monument, the Yampa is a river well worth preserving for generations to come.

Kidney beans six 15-ounce cans, with liquid
Worcestershire sauce 2 teaspoons
Tabasco 1 teaspoon
Honey 2 tablespoons
Tomato paste one 6-ounce can
Dry mustard, garlic powder, and black pepper 1 teaspoon each
Medium bell pepper 1, chopped
Medium yellow onions 2, chopped
Sharp Cheddar cheese ½ pound, grated

Stir Worcestershire sauce, Tabasco, honey, tomato paste, and spices into cooked beans. Pour half of bean mixture into a heated, well-seasoned 10-inch Dutch oven. Place bell pepper, onions, then cheese on top of beans. Top with rest of mixture, bell pepper, and onions. Bake 40 minutes with 6 briquets underneath and 13 on top for a medium oven. When baking time has elapsed, carefully remove lid without disturbing coals. Add remaining cheese. Cover and bake 5 minutes to allow cheese to melt and toast lightly. Serve.

Lodore Enchilada Pie

Serves 6
Preparation time: 1 hour

The Gates of Lodore form the entrance to another beautiful desert canyon on the Green River. Located in the northeast corner of Colorado in Dinosaur National Park, Lodore Canyon has challenging rapids, beautiful scenery, and an abundance of cottonwood trees for shade.

Corn tortillas   8
Pinto beans   four 15-ounce cans
Red onion   1 medium, chopped
Chopped black olives   four 4-ounce cans
Enchilada sauce   three 10-ounce cans
Cheddar cheese   1 pound, grated
Sour cream   1 pint

Place 4 tortillas on bottom of well-oiled 10-inch Dutch oven. Layer half the beans, onions, olives, enchilada sauce, and cheese, in that order, on top of tortillas. Make a second layer on top of first by repeating entire process. Bake 40 minutes with 5 briquets underneath and 15 on top for a medium-hot oven. Serve. Top with sour cream.

Desolation Canyon Garbanzo Curry

Serves 6
Preparation time: 1¼ hours

Beginning this run at Sand Wash, Utah, the Green River flows through the desert country of Desolation Canyon. It was well named by Major John Wesley Powell, for the walls are stark and high, dwarfing the people and boats that drift slowly below.

Garbanzo beans four 15-ounce cans
Whole peeled tomatoes 28-ounce can, chopped
Medium yellow onions 2, chopped
Medium potatoes 4, diced
Garlic cloves 6, minced
Water ½ cup
Curry powder, cumin, turmeric, ginger,
    cayenne pepper, and black pepper to taste
Pineapple chunks 8-ounce can, drained
Raisins 1 cup
Basic Brown Rice (see Index) 6 cups

Combine beans, tomatoes (both with their liquid), onions, potatoes, garlic, water, and spices in large pot. Cover. Simmer 30 minutes or until potatoes are tender. Stir in pineapple and raisins, heating an additional 5 minutes. Serve over rice.

Noodle-Cheese-Nut Thing

Serves 6
Preparation time: 40 minutes

This is one of the first river dishes I learned to make, so it brings back memories of many different river trips.

Salt ¼ teaspoon
Water 4 cups
Oil 1 tablespoon
Elbow noodles 1 pound
Cheddar cheese ¾ pound, grated
Cream of mushroom soup three 10-ounce cans
Unsalted peanuts 1 cup
Shelled sunflower seeds 1 cup
Cashew pieces 1 cup
Curry powder, cumin, turmeric, black pepper,
    cayenne pepper, and dry mustard to taste

Bring salted water and oil to boil. (Oil keeps the noodles from sticking together.) Add noodles. Cook 5 minutes or until tender. Drain off half the water. Stir in remaining ingredients. Heat slowly. Serve.

Simple Spaghetti from Scratch

Serves 6
Preparation time: 1 hour

Olive oil   ¼ cup
Garlic cloves   3, minced
Mushrooms   1 cup chopped
Medium yellow onion   1, chopped
Tomato paste   two 8-ounce cans
Water   2 cups
Salt   ½ teaspoon
Black pepper and garlic powder   1 teaspoon each
Bay leaves   3
Oregano, basil, thyme, and parsley flakes   1 tablespoon each
Salt   ¼ teaspoon
Water   4 cups
Oil   1 tablespoon
Spaghetti noodles   1 pound
Jack cheese   1 pound, grated

Heat olive oil in saucepan. Sauté garlic, mushrooms, and onion until tender. Add tomato paste, 2 cups water, spices, and herbs. Cover and simmer slowly 30 minutes. Add water if sauce is too thick. While sauce is cooking, bring 4 cups salted water and oil to a boil. Add spaghetti. Cook 5 minutes or until tender. Drain. Serve sauce over noodles and top with ample helpings of cheese.

Southwest Vegie Stew

Serves 4
Preparation time: 1 hour

Oil   4 tablespoons
Yellow onion   1 medium, chopped
Garlic   2 cloves, minced
Bell pepper   1 medium, cored and thinly sliced
Potato   1 small, peeled and diced
Carrot   1 large, quartered and sliced
Paprika   ½ teaspoon
Cayenne   ¼ teaspoon
Quick brown or white rice   1 cup (uncooked)
Whole canned tomatoes   one 16-ounce can

Chicken broth one 14-ounce can
Zucchini 1 medium, quartered and sliced
Peas one 15-ounce can, drained

Slice, dice, and chop vegetables. Set aside. Heat oil in large saucepan. Sauté onion and garlic 1 minute. Add bell pepper, potato, carrots, paprika, and cayenne. Cook, stirring, for 5 minutes. Stir in rice, tomatoes, and chicken broth, and bring to a boil. Cover and simmer 20 minutes. Add zucchini and peas. Cook another 10 minutes. Serve.

Snakebite Smith's Eggplant Parmesan

Serves 8
Preparation time: 1 hour

Wesley, as he is more commonly known, received this nickname because of his excellent handling of a rattlesnake bite victim. He is an eleven-year veteran boatman with Arizona Raft Adventures (AzRA) in the Grand Canyon, but this was the first time he had occasion to treat such a bite—which happened shortly after we finished this delicious dinner.

Large eggplant 1
Italian-style zucchini two 16-ounce cans
Mushrooms 16-ounce can, drained
Sliced black olives 4-ounce can, drained
Tomato paste two 8-ounce cans
Ricotta cheese ¼ pound
Mozzarella cheese ½ pound, thinly sliced
Black pepper and garlic powder 1 teaspoon each
Basil, thyme, parsley flakes, and oregano 2 teaspoons each
Parmesan cheese 8 ounces, grated

Cut eggplant crosswise into thin slices and place in bottom of a large, well-oiled frying pan or griddle. Layer zucchini, mushrooms, olives, tomato paste, cheeses, and spices and herbs on top of eggplant. Cover. Cook slowly 45 minutes. Serve accompanied by Parmesan cheese.

Cataract Canyon Lasagna

Serves 6
Preparation time: 45 minutes

Cataract Canyon lies just beyond the confluence of the Green and Colorado rivers in Utah. Suddenly the lazy, quiet rivers become a caldron of huge rapids. It was these big drops that caused Major John Wesley Powell to give this canyon its name.

Salt ¼ teaspoon
Water 4 cups
Oil 1 tablespoon
Lasagna noodles ½ pound
Spinach three 15-ounce cans, drained
Medium yellow onions 2, chopped
Garlic cloves 5, minced
Tomato paste two 8-ounce cans
Black pepper and garlic powder 1 teaspoon each
Oregano, basil, thyme, and parsley flakes 2 teaspoons each
Mozzarella cheese ¾ pound, sliced
Parmesan cheese 8 ounces, grated

Bring salted water and oil to boil. Add lasagna noodles. Cook 5 minutes. Place noodles in thick layer over bottom of well-oiled frying pan or griddle. Layer spinach, onions, garlic, tomato paste, spices, herbs, and mozzarella cheese, in that order, on top of noodles. Cover. Heat slowly 30 minutes. Serve topped with Parmesan cheese.

Dwight's Pizza

Yield: 10-inch pie
Preparation time: 45 minutes

The last night of a particularly memorable Grand Canyon trip, Dwight and I made a special dinner for the group. We arranged a sit-down dinner for sixteen on a white sand beach, using decks as tables. In addition to the scheduled meal, Dwight added this pizza to the menu. Both the evening and the pizza were great successes.

Bisquick   2 cups
Cold water   ½ cup
Tomato sauce   8-ounce can
Medium yellow onion   1, chopped
Diced green chilies   7-ounce can
Sliced mushrooms   4-ounce can, drained
Sliced black olives   4-ounce can, drained
Garlic powder and onion powder   ½ teaspoon each
Black pepper   ¼ teaspoon
Mozzarella cheese   ¼ pound, grated

Mix Bisquick with water to form a firm dough. Place in a well-seasoned 10-inch Dutch oven. Spread tomato sauce, onion, chilies, mushrooms, and black olives over top of dough. Add spices. Sprinkle cheese over top of pizza. Bake 30 minutes with 6 briquets underneath and 13 on top for a medium oven.

Potato Cheese Bake

Serves 8
Preparation time: 1½ to 2 hours

There are two ways to prepare this dish using the same ingredients. One results in a potato soufflé, while the other suggests potatoes au gratin. Both are suitable main dishes.

Medium potatoes   10
Water   1 cup
Milk powder   ½ cup
Eggs   4, beaten
White onions   2, chopped
Swiss cheese   1 pound, grated
Black pepper   ½ teaspoon
Parsley flakes and tarragon   1 tablespoon each
Garlic powder   1 teaspoon

Potato Soufflé: Wash potatoes in clear water and cut into small pieces. Boil potatoes 30 minutes or until tender. Drain off water. Combine water and milk powder. Mash potatoes with milk. Stir in eggs, onions, cheese, spices, and herbs. Pour mixture into a heated, well-oiled 10-inch Dutch oven. Bake 45 minutes with 6 briquets underneath and 13 on top for a medium oven.

Potatoes au Gratin: Wash potatoes in clear water and slice very thin. Layer potato slices alternately with onions and cheese in a well-oiled 10-inch Dutch oven. Combine eggs, milk powder, water, spices, and herbs and pour over potatoes, onions, and cheese. Bake 1½ hours with 6 briquets underneath and 15 on top for a hot oven.

San Juan Summer Squash

Serves 8
Preparation time: 1 hour

The San Juan River in southeastern Utah meanders past petroglyphs, Anasazi cliff dwellings, and around the Goosenecks. It is a place to unwind, lie back, and enjoy the lazy flow and small Edens tucked away in side canyons.

Yellow summer squash (crookneck squash) 5
Milk powder ½ cup
Water 1½ cups
Whole wheat flour 1 cup
Medium yellow onions 2, chopped
Mushrooms ½ pound, sliced
Cheddar cheese ½ pound, grated

Wash squash in clear water and boil 10 minutes. While squash is cooking, combine milk powder with water and heat slowly over a low fire. Add flour gradually to milk, stirring constantly until mixture is syrupy thick and smooth. Remove squash from water and cut in half lengthwise. Scoop out seeds from center. Place squash cut side up in a heated, well-oiled 10-inch Dutch oven. Sprinkle onions and mushrooms over squash. Pour milk and flour mixture over vegetables and top with grated cheese. Bake 40 minutes with 6 briquets underneath and 13 on top for a medium oven.

Sheila's Cabbage Casserole

Serves 4
Preparation time: 1¾ hours

Medium green cabbage 1, shredded
Medium tomatoes 2, chopped
Sharp Cheddar cheese 1 pound, grated
Cottage cheese 1 pound
Tomato or V-8 juice ½ cup
Garlic powder ½ teaspoon
Black pepper ¼ teaspoon
Celery seed ½ teaspoon
Basic Brown Rice (see Index) 8 cups

Combine cabbage, tomatoes, cheeses, juice, spices, and herbs with cooked rice. Put mixture in a seasoned, heated 8-inch Dutch oven and bake 35 minutes with 4 briquets underneath and 9 on top for a medium oven. Serve.

Tate Creek Stuffed Peppers

Serves 8
Preparation time: 1¾ hours

Tate Creek is usually the last night's camp on a Rogue River trip. One of the main attractions is a daring waterfall slide a short hike up the creek. When you are perched on top of the waterfall, the drop looks endless, though it is perhaps only twenty feet—half on the slide and half free-falling into a clear, cold pool. It's guaranteed to work up an appetite.

Basic Brown Rice (see Index)   8 cups
Medium yellow onions   2, chopped
Whole peeled tomatoes   two 28-ounce cans, chopped
Garlic clove   1, minced
Black pepper   1 teaspoon
Basil, thyme, and cumin   1 tablespoon each
Chili powder   ¼ teaspoon
Cayenne pepper   pinch
Large bell peppers   8
Jack cheese   1 pound, grated

Mix cooked rice with onions, tomatoes (with juice), garlic, spices, and herbs. Carefully cut center out of each pepper. Spoon rice mixture into peppers. Place in a heated, well-seasoned 10-inch Dutch oven. Keep leftover rice hot at edge of fire or on low flame on stove. Bake peppers 40 minutes with 6 briquets underneath and 13 on top for a medium oven. Sprinkle cheese on top of peppers and leftover rice. Serve.

Flambeau River Welsh Rabbit

Serves 6
Preparation time: 20 minutes

The Flambeau River in north central Wisconsin received its name from French explorers who came upon a group of Indians fishing by torchlight along its banks. It offers a scenic float through thick forests for canoeists and rafters. In a state known for its beer and cheese, this is an appropriate dish.

Water to fill bottom of double boiler
Butter 1 tablespoon
Beer 1 cup
Sharp Cheddar cheese 2 pounds, grated
Worcestershire sauce 2 teaspoons
Dry mustard ½ teaspoon
Cayenne pepper, paprika, curry powder, cumin, and turmeric ¼ teaspoon each
Bread 1 loaf, sliced

Create a double boiler by placing a smaller pan inside a larger one. Put water in larger pan and bring to a boil. Melt butter in smaller pan. Stir in beer. When beer is warm, add cheese. As cheese melts, stir in Worcestershire sauce and spices. At the same time, toast slices of bread on grill over fire or in frying pan with butter. Pour rabbit over toast. Serve immediately.
Variation: A more substantial dish can be achieved by adding spinach or asparagus. Heat contents of two 15-ounce cans of either vegetable. Drain well and place directly on toast. Pour rabbit over vegetable and toast.

Salmon River Quiche

Serves 8
Preparation time: 1½ hours

The Salmon River in Idaho runs through the second deepest gorge in North America. Deemed unnavigable by Captain Clark of the Lewis and Clark expedition, it was declared the "river of no return." No longer considered even very difficult, it is a popular run with moderate rapids, sandy beaches, and warm water ideal for swimming.

Salt   ¼ teaspoon
Whole wheat flour   1½ cups
Oil   2 tablespoons
Cold water   ⅓ cup
Eggs   8, beaten
White onion   1, chopped
Milk powder   ¼ cup
Water   1 cup
Chopped black olives   two 4-ounce cans, drained
Diced green chilies   two 4-ounce cans
Swiss cheese   ¾ pound, grated
Black pepper and dry mustard   ½ teaspoon each

Stir salt into flour. Blend oil in thoroughly with a fork. Add ⅓ cup water, a few drops at a time, until dough holds together easily. Roll out with a glass jar and put into a heated, well-seasoned 10-inch Dutch oven. Combine remaining ingredients in bowl and pour into pie shell. Bake 1 hour with 6 briquets underneath and 13 on top for a medium oven.

Beans Amandine

Serves 6
Preparation time: 30 minutes

This quick and easy recipe is ideal for rainy weather or anytime you want a meal in a hurry.

Salt   ¼ teaspoon
Water   4 cups
Oil   1 tablespoon
Elbow noodles   1 pound
French-style green beans   three 16-ounce cans
Cream of mushroom soup   two 10-ounce cans
Almonds   1 cup slivered
Black pepper   ¼ teaspoon
Basil, garlic powder, and oregano   ½ teaspoon each

Bring lightly salted water and oil to a boil. Add noodles. Cook 5 minutes or until tender. Combine remaining ingredients and herbs and spices in separate saucepan and heat slowly, stirring to keep from sticking. Serve over noodles.
Variation: Rice may be substituted for noodles, but will add to preparation time.

Falafel Burgers

Yield: four 5-inch patties
Preparation time: 30 minutes

Water   1½ cups
Falafel mix   2 cups
Oil   ⅓ cup
English muffins   4
Small red onion   1, sliced
Tomatoes   2, sliced
Cucumber   1, peeled and sliced
Sprouts   1 cup
Mayonnaise   8-ounce jar
Dijon mustard   8-ounce jar
Garlic powder, parsley flakes, and black pepper   to taste

Add water gradually to falafel mix. Let mixture stand 15 minutes to absorb water completely. Form into four 5-inch patties. Heat oil in a frying pan over medium heat. Sauté falafel patties 5 minutes on each side until golden brown. When done, place burgers on paper towel to absorb grease. Lightly toast English muffins. Serve patties on muffins topped with onion, tomato, cucumber, sprouts, mayonnaise, mustard, spices, and parsley.
Note: Falafel mix may be purchased in bulk or packaged form at health food stores.

Doug's Soyburgers

Yield: eight 5-inch patties
Preparation time: 1 hour

Doug originally made these delicious burgers with soybeans. I prefer using soy grits as they take less time to prepare.

Dry soy grits   2 cups
Rolled oats   2 cups
Whole wheat flour   ⅓ cup
Large eggs   3
Tamari or soy sauce   2 tablespoons
Black pepper   ½ teaspoon
Garlic powder   1 teaspoon
Oil   for frying
Small red onion   1, thinly sliced
Cheddar cheese   ½ pound, sliced
Sprouts   garnish
Mayonnaise, ketchup, steak sauce, salsa jalapeña

Prepare soy grits according to instructions for Basic Beans (see Index). Combine cooked soy grits with oats, flour, eggs, tamari, and spices. Form into patties. Heat a thin layer of oil in frying pan. Add patties. Cover. Cook slowly 30 minutes, turning once. When burgers are nearly done, top each patty with onion and cheese slices. Cover. Heat until cheese has melted. Serve with sprouts and selected sauces.

Eel River Tostados

Serves 8
Preparation time: 40 minutes

Mention of the Eel River brings memories of a morning heavy with fog, a dinner celebrated by a double rainbow, an otter swimming Coal Mine Falls, an outrageous wrap on an unnamed rock, a race with the dark to take-out, and an exceptional group of people.

Refried beans   three 17-ounce cans
Large red onion   1, chopped
Avocado   1, peeled and pitted
Tomatoes   3, chopped
Cheddar or Jack cheese   1 pound, grated
Corn or flour tortillas   16
Black pepper and garlic powder   to taste
Sprouts   garnish
Salsa jalapeña   8-ounce jar

Heat beans in saucepan. Arrange onion, avocado, tomatoes, and cheese on a plate and set near stove or fire. Heat a single tortilla for 1 or 2 minutes on 1 side in a lightly oiled skillet. Turn. Place a large spoonful of beans on tortilla. Add onion, spices, and cheese. Cover skillet and heat 1 or 2 minutes until cheese melts. Transfer to a plate. Add avocado, tomatoes, and sprouts. Top with salsa jalapeña to taste.

Rain's Chili con Chilies

Serves 6
Preparation time: 1 to 2 hours

Rain (he really prefers to be called Jeff) is definitely one of the more colorful people running rivers. We have shared the highs and lows of many trips, and I still never know what he might do next. Whether he comes up with something outrageous or something down-to-earth, he adds a spark of vitality to every trip.

Oil
Medium yellow onion   1, sliced
Garlic cloves   3, minced
Kidney beans   four 15-ounce cans
Diced green chilies   three 7-ounce cans
Whole peeled tomatoes   one 24-ounce can, chopped
Tomato paste   one 6-ounce can
Chili powder and black pepper   to taste
Cheddar cheese   ½ pound, grated

Heat a thin layer of oil in large saucepan. Sauté onions and garlic. Add beans, chilies, tomato paste, and tomatoes with their juices to onions and garlic. Add spices. Simmer 30 minutes. Serve, topping each bowl with grated cheese.

Tuolumne Rellenos

Serves 4
Preparation time: 1¼ hours

Some of my most memorable trips have been on the Tuolumne River in the Sierra foothills of California. The Tuolumne is full of legendary rapids and stories to go with them, beautiful side creeks, and lovely campsites where many evenings have been spent around the campfire telling river stories.

Cheddar cheese   1 pound
Whole green chilies   four 7-ounce cans, drained
Eggs   8, separated
Whole wheat flour   1 cup
Black pepper, cumin, and cayenne pepper   to taste

Slice cheese into 2-inch chunks ¼-inch thick. Slit chilies lengthwise and put cheese inside. Combine egg yolks with flour and spices. Beat egg whites until stiff. (Since this takes considerable time and energy, pass the bowl among the kitchen crew so the job does not become tedious for one person.) Add beaten whites to yolks, flour, and spices. Layer half the chilies in a heated, well-oiled 10-inch Dutch oven. Pour half the egg mixture over chilies. Layer remaining chilies on top of egg mixture and pour rest of egg batter over top. Bake 45 minutes with 6 briquets underneath and 13 on top for a medium oven.

BEAST, FOWL, AND FISH

Barbecued Steaks, Hamburgers, and Chicken

Preparation time: 20 minutes to 1¼ hours

Barbecued meat and poultry are traditional favorites of campers and are about the easiest meals of all to prepare.

Frying chicken, cut up   1 whole chicken for 3 people
New York cut steaks   1 per person
Prime ground beef   ¼ pound per person
Barbecue sauce, steak sauce, Tabasco,
     Worcestershire sauce, tamari, or soy sauce
Salt, black pepper, garlic powder, and onion powder   to taste

A hot fire is necessary to barbecue meat. Charcoal briquets give off intense heat and eliminate the need to wait for a large fire to die down before cooking over coals. Don't try cooking over high flames or you'll end up with charred meat.

Boil chicken whole 15 minutes to speed up cooking time. When coals are ready, put meat on grill. Coat each side with selected sauces and spices. Cook chicken about 45 minutes, turning once. Grill steaks and hamburgers to suit individual tastes.

Saint Croix Meat Loaf

Serves 8
Preparation time: 1¼ hours

The Saint Croix River glides through thick forests of maple and hemlock, forming a natural border between Maine and New Brunswick, Canada. With only one rapid of any difficulty, this is a peaceful, easy two-day run through beautiful country.

Eggs   2, lightly beaten
Lean ground beef   2 pounds
Fresh bread crumbs   2 cups
Medium yellow onion   1, chopped
Bell pepper   1, chopped
Tomato sauce   8-ounce can
Ketchup   ½ cup
Horseradish   2 tablespoons
Black pepper and dry mustard   ½ teaspoon each
Basil, celery seed, and dill seed   1 teaspoon each

Stir meat, crumbs, onions, and pepper into eggs. Add tomato sauce, ketchup, horseradish, spices, and herbs. Mix thoroughly with as few strokes as possible. Pour into a heated, well-seasoned 10-inch Dutch oven. Spread a thin layer of ketchup over top of meat loaf. Bake 1 hour with 6 briquets underneath and 15 on top for a medium-hot oven. Serve.

Hells Canyon Stroganoff

Serves 8
Preparation time: 1 hour

Hells Canyon, the deepest gorge in North America, earned its name through the combination of wild water, intense heat, and the blackness of its inner gorge. This is a beautiful trip, combining good white water with slow river days and time for hiking.

Sirloin strips   3 pounds
Whole wheat flour   1 cup
Oil   for frying
Medium yellow onion   1, chopped
Mushrooms   ½ pound, chopped
Cream of mushroom soup   10-ounce can
Sour cream   1 pint
Black pepper, garlic powder, basil, and nutmeg   to taste
Salt   ¼ teaspoon
Water   4 cups
Oil   1 tablespoon
Egg noodles   1 pound

Roll sirloin strips in flour. Heat a thin layer of oil in a large frying pan, griddle, or saucepan. Brown sirloin with onions and mushrooms. Remove from fire. Stir in soup, sour cream, spices, and basil. Heat slowly over a low fire. While this is cooking, bring salted water and oil to a boil. Add noodles. Cook until tender. Serve stroganoff over noodles.

Klamath River Beef Stew

Serves 8
Preparation time: 1¼ hours

Flowing through Sasquatch territory, the Klamath River in northern California is a gentle river with easy rapids. Osprey and great blue heron are abundant and you may hear the sounds of "Bigfoot" at night.

Oil   for frying
Sirloin tip   2 pounds, cubed
Whole wheat flour   1 cup
Medium potatoes   4, cubed
Medium carrots   6, chopped
White onions   6
Whole tomatoes with juice   16-ounce can, chopped
Onion soup mix   1 envelope
Beef broth   14-ounce can
Water   1 cup
Black pepper, garlic powder, basil, bay leaves,
    thyme, and parsley flakes   to taste

Place thin layer of oil in large saucepan and heat over a medium fire. Roll sirloin in flour and brown in hot oil. When sirloin is browned, add vegetables, soup mix, beef broth, water, spices, and herbs. Simmer over a medium fire 45 minutes. Serve.

Beef or Lamb Kebabs

Serves 8
Preparation time: 1¾ hours

This meal has a certain elegance to it, and the advantage of being very easy to prepare.

Sirloin tip or lamb shoulder   2 pounds
Tamari   1 cup
Wine vinegar or red wine   1 cup
Parsley flakes, thyme, oregano, basil,
    tarragon, and rosemary   1 teaspoon each

Cherry tomatoes   1-pound box
Whole peeled potatoes   20-ounce can
Large green peppers   2, sliced
Large red onion   1, cut in eighths
Fresh pineapple   1, cut in chunks
Skewers   8
Black pepper, garlic powder, and onion powder   to taste
Barbecue sauce, Worcestershire sauce, or tamari

Cut meat into 2-inch chunks. Combine tamari, wine vinegar, and herbs in bowl. Add meat and marinate for 1 hour. Arrange tomatoes, potatoes, slices of pepper, pieces of onion, and chunks of pineapple on plates. Set near fire with skewers, spices, and sauces. When meat has marinated a while, have everyone make up his or her own skewer and cook over a hot bed of coals 10 to 20 minutes, turning frequently.

Briggs's Beans

Serves 8
Preparation time: 1¼ hours

Tall, lanky, boatman Don Briggs discovered this meal many years ago. Due to some skepticism about its value for a commercial menu, the dish was given his name so he might take the blame—and the praise, as it turned out.

Batter for New River Cornbread (see Index)   1 recipe
Bacon   1 pound
Ranch-style beans   three 16-ounce cans
Large red onion   1, chopped
Molasses   ¼ cup
Brown sugar   ¼ cup
Ketchup   3 tablespoons

Traditionally the cornbread for this recipe has been made pancake-style. Thin out the batter by adding water and fry on a griddle. It's faster and easier than baking.

Put bacon in a large saucepan and fry until it is about three-quarters done. Drain off grease. Stir in beans, onion, molasses, brown sugar, and ketchup. Heat slowly over a low to medium fire 15 minutes, stirring frequently or until mixture is hot. Serve over cornbread pancakes.

Bass Camp Sweet and Sour Ham

Serves 8
Preparation time: 45 minutes

William Bass came to the Southwest in the late 1880s to rid himself of tuber-culosis. Having no success with mining in the Grand Canyon, he developed a tourist business leading people between Rim and River, leaving behind his name at this beautiful camp.

Ham   4-pound can
Dijon mustard   to taste
Whole cloves   4
Bell peppers   2, sliced
Pineapple rings   20-ounce can
Sweet and sour sauce   8-ounce jar

Thinly slice ham and layer in bottom of a 10-inch Dutch oven. Add mustard, cloves, bell pepper, pineapple with juice, and sweet and sour sauce on top of ham. Bake 30 minutes with 6 briquets underneath and 15 on top for a hot oven. Serve.

Deschutes Chicken Curry

Serves 4
Preparation time: 1¼ hours

The Deschutes River in north central Oregon is a popular boating river with fine examples of volcanic action that took place in that vicinity about fifty million years ago. The Deschutes so impressed French fur trappers when they came upon the river where it pours over Celilo Falls into the Columbia that they named it "river of falls."

Basic Brown Rice (see Index)   4 cups
Whole chicken   50-ounce can
Green peas   17-ounce can, drained
Cashew pieces   1 cup
Curry powder, cumin, turmeric, ginger,
    cayenne pepper, and black pepper   to taste
Chutney   8-ounce jar

While rice is cooking, bone chicken and cut into small pieces. Add chicken, some of its juice, peas, cashews, and spices to cooked rice. Heat thoroughly. Serve with chutney on side.

Tamari Chicken

Serves 4
Preparation time: 1 hour

Frying chicken 1 whole, cut up
Water 1 cup
Crushed pineapple 8-ounce can
Tamari ¼ cup
Medium yellow onion 1, chopped
Medium bell pepper 1, chopped
Almonds 1 cup slivered
Black pepper and dry mustard ½ teaspoon each

Place chicken in large frying pan with water, juice from pineapple, and tamari. Cover and steam 20 minutes over a medium fire. Turn chicken and add onions, green pepper, almonds, and spices. Cover and steam another 20 minutes or until most of liquid is gone. Add pineapple, heating slightly. Serve.

Tom's Baked Chicken

Serves 8
Preparation time: 1¼ hours

This recipe is a good example of what a well-stocked spice and staples box can do. Instead of making fried chicken as the menu called for, Tom concocted this recipe after we arrived at camp. The results are unbelievably delicious.

Oil for frying
Frying chickens 2 whole, cut up
Tamari 1 cup
Wine vinegar 3 tablespoons
Water 2 cups
Parsley flakes, thyme, oregano, basil, tarragon, and rosemary
    1 teaspoon each
Black pepper ½ teaspoon

Heat oil in a 10-inch Dutch oven. Lightly brown chicken on both sides. When all chicken pieces are browned, add tamari, wine vinegar, water, herbs, and pepper. Bake 45 minutes with 6 briquets underneath and 13 on top for a medium-hot oven. Serve.

Cherry Creek Chicken

Serves 4
Preparation time: 1¼ hours

Cherry Creek and the Upper Tuolumne in the central Sierra were considered unrunnable in a raft (and still might be by some) until recently. With vertical drops through narrow chutes, the boatman must take precise strokes to keep the raft from flipping. Passengers who sign up for this trip must pass a physical fitness test and have prior white-water experience. This elegant dish is suitable for celebrating a successful run of such a challenging stretch.

Oil   for frying
Frying chicken   1 whole, cut up
Tarragon and parsley flakes   1 tablespoon each
Black pepper and garlic powder   1 teaspoon each
Mushrooms   ¼ pound, quartered
Medium yellow onion   1, chopped
White wine   1 cup
Sour cream   ½ pint

Pour a thin layer of oil in a large frying pan and heat over a medium fire. When hot, add chicken, browning lightly on both sides. As each side browns, add herbs and spices. Reduce heat, cover, and sauté chicken 20 minutes on 1 side. Turn chicken and add mushrooms and onion. Sauté another 20 minutes. Uncover and drain excess oil. Add wine and bring to a high simmer. Cook 5 minutes, turning chicken frequently. Add sour cream and simmer another 5 minutes. Serve.

Orange Almond Chicken

Serves 4
Preparation time: 1 hour

Oil
Fryer chicken 1 whole, cut up
Flour 3 tablespoons
Raisins 1 cup
Cinnamon ½ teaspoon
Tamari 1 tablespoon
Brown sugar 1 tablespoon
Tabasco sauce 8 drops
Orange juice 1¼ cups
Orange 1, sectioned
Almonds ½ cup, slivered

Brown both sides of chicken in oil in large skillet. Remove and set aside. Stir flour, cinnamon, tamari, brown sugar, and Tabasco sauce in pan with drippings until smooth. Stir in orange juice and bring to a boil. Add chicken and raisins. Cover and simmer over low heat 30 to 40 minutes. Add orange sections and almonds, cook 5 minutes. Serve.

Shrimp Fried Rice

Serves 8
Preparation time: 1½ hours

Medium white onions 2, chopped
Oil 1 to 2 tablespoons
Basic Brown Rice (see Index) 8 cups
Canned deveined shrimp four 4-ounce cans, drained
Peas two 15-ounce cans, drained
Water chestnuts two 7-ounce cans, drained and chopped
Eggs 4, beaten
Tamari ½ cup
Black pepper ½ teaspoon
Cayenne pepper ¼ teaspoon

Brown onions in large frying pan or on griddle over a low to medium fire. Stir in cooked rice, shrimp, peas, water chestnuts, and eggs. Add tamari and spices, stirring constantly. Cook until mixture is lightly browned. Serve.

McKenzie Fish Fillets

Serves 8
Preparation time: 40 minutes

Flowing through the timbered lands of the Willamette National Forest, the McKenzie is one of Oregon's most beautiful rivers. The McKenzie is noted for its excellent fishing, which gave birth to the McKenzie River Boat. This drift boat, which is slightly different from the Grand Canyon Dory, was designed here by McKenzie guides to be used especially for drift fishing.

Fish fillets (turbot, perch, butterfish, flounder, sole)   3 pounds
Black pepper   ½ teaspoon
Garlic powder   1 teaspoon
Tarragon and parsley flakes   1 tablespoon each
Water
Butter
Lemon

Wash fish in clear water. Season with spices and herbs. Place in frying pan or griddle. Cover bottom of pan with ⅛-inch layer of water. Bring water to boil and immediately reduce heat. Cover pan and simmer about 10 minutes, turning fish once. While fish is cooking, melt butter and cut lemon into wedges. Serve with melted butter and lemon wedges on side.

Baked Fish Fillets

Serves 6
Preparation time: 30 minutes

Fish fillets (turbot, perch, butterfish, flounder, sole)   2 pounds
Dry white wine   1 cup
Sour cream   ½ pint
Paprika   ½ teaspoon
Parsley flakes   1 tablespoon

Place fish fillets in a 10-inch heated Dutch oven seasoned with butter. Pour wine over fillets. Add sour cream, paprika, and parsley on top. Bake 20 minutes with 6 briquets underneath and 15 on top for a hot oven. Serve.

Kern River Red Snapper

Serves 8
Preparation time: 45 minutes

The Kern River in the southern Sierra of California offers three exciting white-water runs. The most difficult of these, the Forks of the Kern, was first descended by raft in 1980. The beginning of this high-altitude trip is unique for the only access is via a three-mile trail. While people carry their own gear, mules pack in rafts.

Medium yellow onion   1, chopped
Garlic cloves   4, minced
Whole tomatoes   28-ounce can, drained
Salsa Casera   7-ounce can
Diced green chilies   two 4-ounce cans, drained
Oregano and parsley flakes   1 tablespoon each
Cornstarch   ¼ cup
Large lemons   2
Water   ¼ cup (or less)
Red snapper fillets   3 pounds

Sauté onion and garlic in a saucepan until lightly browned. Chop tomatoes and add to onion and garlic along with Salsa Casera, chilies, and herbs. Cook over moderate heat until sauce thickens. Meanwhile, mix cornstarch, lemon juice and pulp, and water to a syrupy smoothness. Stir into sauce. Heat a frying pan or griddle over medium heat and place red snapper fillets flat in pan. Pour sauce over fillets and cook about 20 minutes, turning once. Serve.

Chattooga Southern-Fried Catfish

Preparation time: 20 minutes

Descending through the Great Smokey Mountains, the Chattooga is a beautiful and exciting river, demanding high skills from boaters. The Chattooga achieved national fame when scenes from the movie Deliverance *were shot there. It is now included in the Wild and Scenic Rivers system, thus protecting it from future development.*

Catfish   1 per person
Black pepper   ¼ teaspoon
Basil and thyme   ½ teaspoon each
Cornmeal   ¼ cup
Oil   for frying

Clean and skin catfish. Stir pepper and herbs into cornmeal, and coat fish with cornmeal. Cover the bottom of a frying pan with oil ¼-inch deep. Heat over a hot fire. Fry catfish until golden brown. Serve.

Tatshenshini Salmon Steaks

Serves 8
Preparation time: 1½ hours

Beginning in Canada's Yukon Territory and flowing southwest to the Gulf of Alaska, the Tatshenshini is a spectacular river. With lively rapids, thick forests, bald eagles, moose, snowcapped mountains, fields of flowers, and endless summer days, it's easy to think you're in heaven—except perhaps for the mosquitoes, flies, and maybe a surprise visit from a grizzly.

Red wine   ¾ cup
Olive oil   ¾ cup
Medium lemon   1
Tamari or soy sauce   1 tablespoon
Black pepper   ½ teaspoon
Thyme and sage   1 teaspoon each
Parsley flakes and tarragon   1 tablespoon each
Salmon steaks   8

Combine wine, oil, juice and pulp of lemon, tamari, pepper, and herbs in a large flat dish or pan. Marinate salmon steaks in sauce 1 to 3 hours. Cook steaks on grill over charcoal, brushing frequently with marinade. Brown on both sides, turning carefully, and cook until tender, about 15 minutes. Serve.

Baked Salmon Loaf

Serves 6
Preparation time: 1 hour

Salmon   two 16-ounce cans
Milk powder   ¼ cup
Water   1 cup
Small yellow onion   1, chopped
Eggs   2, beaten
Bread   4 slices, crumbled
Black pepper   ¼ teaspoon
Garlic powder   ½ teaspoon
Parsley flakes   1 teaspoon
Butter   3 tablespoons
Flour   2½ tablespoons
Milk powder   ½ cup
Water   1½ cups
Jack cheese   ½ pound, grated
Paprika   ¼ teaspoon
Cayenne pepper   pinch

Put salmon and its liquid into a bowl. Mix ¼ cup milk powder with 1 cup water and add to salmon. Add next 6 ingredients to salmon, mixing thoroughly. Pour mixture into a heated, well-seasoned 10-inch Dutch oven. Bake 45 minutes with 6 briquets underneath and 13 on top for a medium oven. While loaf is baking, prepare sauce. Melt butter in small pan. Stir in flour gradually until smooth. Mix ½ cup milk powder with 1½ cups water and add to mixture. When hot, stir in cheese and beat to keep smooth. Add remaining spices. Serve over salmon loaf.

Note: If you don't have bread available, tortillas, muffins, biscuits, or crackers may be substituted. Or buy a 16-ounce can or box of bread crumbs.

North Umpqua Trout

Preparation time: 30 minutes

The North Fork of the Umpqua River in western Oregon is a river that laughs. As it plays its way over rocks and around boulders, it forms small drops and slalom courses. A thick evergreen forest rises on both sides of the river, and fly anglers frequent the banks.

Trout
Butter   ½ cup
Garlic powder, onion powder, tarragon, and parsley flakes   to taste
Lemon   1

Catch trout. (This may extend preparation time slightly.) Clean trout and place each on piece of aluminum foil large enough to wrap around fish. Put thin slices of butter both inside and outside of trout. Season with spices and herbs. Wrap foil completely around trout and place on grate over a low to medium fire. Cook 15 or 20 minutes, turning once. Test fish with a fork. Flesh should be flaky. Serve with lemon wedge on side.

Clam Linguine

Serves 4
Preparation time: 20 minutes

Water
Linguine   1 pound
Margarine   ¼ cup
Garlic   2 cloves, minced
Clams   three 10-ounce cans
Flour   2 tablespoons
Black pepper, thyme, parsley   to taste
Parmesan cheese   one 8-ounce can

Bring water to boil in large saucepan. Add linguine. While linguine is cooking, melt margarine in second pan. Add garlic and cook 2 minutes. Stir in clams, flour, black pepper, and herbs. Continue stirring over low heat. When linguine is tender, drain off water and top with clam sauce. Sprinkle with parmesan cheese.

SWEET
TREATS

Laura's Carob-Sesame Balls

Yield: twenty-four 1-inch balls
Preparation time: 1 hour

Butter   ½ cup
Honey   2 tablespoons
Vanilla   ½ teaspoon
Carob powder   ½ cup
Milk powder   ½ cup
Sesame seeds   1 cup

Blend butter and honey until creamy. Add vanilla. Combine carob and milk powders. Add to butter mixture. Add sesame seeds and mix well. Shape into teaspoon-size balls. Place in cooler ½ hour or more.

Variety Sweet Loaf

Yield: 8-inch round loaf
Preparation time: 1½ hours

This loaf lives up to its name by providing a good variety of cakes and breads, all using the same basic ingredients. It is ideal for extended river trips, since the main ingredients can be purchased in bulk and then mixed into different batters once on the river. On short trips, the dry ingredients can be combined ahead of time and carried in a plastic container to save space. In any of its forms it will satisfy a sweet tooth without using sugar and provide some valuable protein.

Whole wheat flour   2 cups
Baking powder   2 teaspoons
Baking soda   1 teaspoon
Milk powder   ⅓ cup
Salt   1 teaspoon
Oil   2 tablespoons
Eggs   2
Vanilla   1 teaspoon
Honey   ½ cup
Desired filling (see individual variations)
Water   1 cup (or less)

Sift flour through a strainer for a lighter, less grainy loaf. Combine first 5 ingredients in a bowl. Add oil, eggs, vanilla, honey, and filling directly to dry ingredients, mixing thoroughly. Slowly stir in water, adding only enough to moisten batter. It should not be too runny, or cake will fall apart when done. Pour into a heated, well-seasoned 8-inch Dutch oven. Bake 1¼ hours with 4 briquets underneath and 9 on top for a medium oven.

Variations:

>for a sweeter, lighter loaf use whole wheat pastry flour in place of regular flour and increase the amount of honey to ¾ cup;

>for banana bread, add 2 or 3 very ripe bananas as filling and bake as directed;

>for pineapple upside-down cake, use pastry flour in place of regular flour and add 8-ounce can of pineapple rings to the list of ingredients; layer pineapple rings on bottom of Dutch oven and pour batter over them; when serving, turn cake bottom-side up;

>for date-nut bread, add 1 cup each of chopped pitted dates and walnuts plus 1 teaspoon of cinnamon to recipe; allow to cool and serve with a cream cheese topping;

>for fruit or berry cake, bake Variety Sweet Loaf plain and serve with a topping of either fresh or canned fruit or berries and whipped cream or sour cream.

Janet's Ukonom Creek Cake

Yield: 8-inch round loaf
Preparation time: 1½ hours

The last night of a river trip can sometimes be either feast or famine, depending on how food has been planned and used. At our final camp along the Klamath River, Janet created this rich, delicious cake out of leftovers.

Chocolate cake mix   1 box
Eggs   as mix calls for
Brandy (optional)   2 tablespoons
Water   as mix calls for
Peaches   6 medium
Heavy cream   ½ pint

Combine cake mix with eggs, brandy, and half the amount of water called for on the package. Slice peaches and place in bottom of a heated, well-seasoned 8-inch Dutch oven. Pour batter over peaches. Bake 1¼ hours with 4 briquets underneath and 9 on top for a medium oven. Serve with cream, either whipped or plain.

Wolf River Yogurt Cake

Yield: 8-inch round loaf
Preparation time: 1 hour and 10 minutes

Narrow and rocky, the Wolf River in northeastern Wisconsin has challenging drops interspersed with stretches of quiet water. When you are not concentrating on one of the many rapids, you can take in the wild, rugged scenery and fish for rainbow, brown, and brook trout.

Cafix, Postum, or Pero   3 tablespoons
Hot water   ¼ cup
Whole wheat pastry flour   2 cups
Baking powder   1 teaspoon
Baking soda   ½ teaspoon
Salt   ¼ teaspoon
Butter or margarine   ½ cup
Honey   ¾ cup
Egg   1
Vanilla   1 teaspoon
Plain yogurt   1 cup

Mix Cafix with hot water and set aside. Combine flour, baking powder, baking soda, and salt in bowl. Soften butter and honey and stir into dry ingredients along with egg, vanilla, and yogurt. Stir in beverage mixture. Pour into a heated, well-oiled 8-inch Dutch oven. Bake 50 minutes with 4 briquets underneath and 9 on top for a medium oven. Serve.
Variation: If you're a coffee lover, use instant coffee in place of cereal beverage, mixing at the same strength.

Peshtigo Cheesecake

Serves 8
Preparation time: 30 minutes

The Peshtigo River in northeastern Wisconsin has two runnable sections and some of the best white water in the state. The upper section, through the Nicolet National Forest, includes numerous mild rapids. The lower part, known as the Roaring Rapids Section, plunges over one drop after another for its entire four-mile length.

Graham crackers ⅔ pound
Butter or margarine ¼ pound, melted
Cream cheese three 8-ounce packages
Eagle Brand sweetened condensed milk 16-ounce can
Lemon 1
Nutmeg and cinnamon ¼ teaspoon each
Pitted sweet cherries 15-ounce can

Crush graham crackers by placing them in a plastic bag and mashing them with a jar, wooden spoon, or other blunt object. Place crumbs in a pie tin, Dutch oven, or large pan. Mix with melted butter to form crust. Combine cream cheese with half of the sweetened condensed milk (save the rest for coffee or tea), juice and pulp of lemon, and spices. Beat with a wire whip until fluffy. Spread over crust. Arrange cherries on top. Chill in a cooler or carefully place bottom of container in cold water. Serve.

Creamy Pumpkin Pie

Yield: 8-inch pie
Preparation time: 1¼ hours

Whole wheat pastry flour 1½ cups
Salt ¼ teaspoon
Oil 2 tablespoons
Cold water ½ cup
Pumpkin 15-ounce can
Eggs 2
Eagle Brand sweetened condensed milk 16-ounce can
Pumpkin pie spice, nutmeg, and cinnamon ¼ teaspoon each
Heavy cream ½ pint
Honey 2 tablespoons

Stir salt into flour. Mix in oil using a fork. Add water, a few drops at a time, until dough holds together easily. Place in bottom of a heated, well-seasoned 8-inch Dutch oven. Combine pumpkin with eggs, half the sweetened condensed milk, and spices. Pour into shell. Bake 1 hour with 4 briquets underneath and 9 on top for a medium oven. Whip cream until thick, adding honey as cream begins to stiffen. Serve pie topped with whipped cream.

Boundary Waters Apple Crisp

Yield: 8-inch pie
Preparation time: 1 hour

In the Boundary Waters Canoe area, canoeists can paddle an entire summer without retracing or even crossing their own trails. The extensive waterways are lined by a large variety of wildlife and a medley of birds nesting in the Boundary Waters Wilderness, which covers over a million acres in northern Minnesota and another million in Canada.

Large apples   8
Graham crackers   ⅔ pound
Butter   ½ cup, melted
Fresh lemon juice   of 1 lemon
Cinnamon and nutmeg   to taste
Brown sugar   ½ cup

Cut apples into small slices and steam or boil 10 minutes or until partially softened. Drain off water. Crush graham crackers by placing them in a plastic bag and mashing them with a blunt object. Place crumbs in a well-seasoned 8-inch Dutch oven. Combine with butter to form crust. Put partially cooked apples on top of crumbs. Squeeze lemon over apples and sprinkle with cinnamon, nutmeg, and brown sugar. Bake 30 minutes with 4 briquets underneath and 9 on top for a medium oven. Serve.

Silver Grotto Sopaipillas

Serves 6 to 8
Preparation time: 1 hour

Undulating walls and a series of pools hide the Silver Grotto on the Colorado River from the casual eye. With some time and climbing ability, however, you can reach this lovely place and pass a special afternoon within its confines.

Whole wheat pastry flour 3 cups
Salt 1 teaspoon
Milk powder ¼ cup
Eggs 2
Water 1 cup
Oil 1½ cups
Honey ¼ cup
Butter ¼ cup, melted

Combine ½ cup of flour with salt and milk powder. Blend in eggs and water. Add remaining flour, a little at a time, until consistency of dough is firm and dry. Dust a cutting board and a glass jar with flour. Separate dough into 3- to 4-inch squares. Heat oil in a deep saucepan and drop squares of dough 1 at a time into very hot oil. The dough will instantly puff up if oil is hot enough. Deep fry until a light golden brown. Transfer sopaipillas to paper towels for draining. Combine honey and butter. Heat. Dip sopaipillas into hot butter and honey mixture.

Rice Pudding

Serves 6
Preparation time: 2 hours

Milk powder ⅓ cup
Water 1¼ cups
Brown sugar ½ cup
Butter 1 tablespoon, softened
Vanilla 1 teaspoon
Eggs 3
Lemon ½
Basic Brown Rice (see Index) 4 cups
Raisins ⅓ cup

Combine milk powder with water. Add brown sugar, butter, vanilla, eggs, and lemon juice and pulp, mixing well. Stir into cooked rice and add raisins. Pour into a heated, well-seasoned 8-inch Dutch oven. Bake 50 minutes with 4 briquets underneath and 9 on top for a medium oven.

Crushed Fruit Tapioca Pudding

Serves 8
Preparation time: 1¼ hours

Water   2 cups
Minute Tapioca   ⅓ cup
Brown sugar   ¾ cup
Crushed pineapple   20-ounce can
Small lemon   1
Whipped cream topping   optional

Bring water to a boil in saucepan. Gradually stir in tapioca and sugar. Bring more water to boil in a second saucepan slightly larger than the first pan. When tapioca and sugar are boiling, place smaller pan in the boiling water of larger pan, creating a double boiler. Cook, stirring constantly, for about 5 minutes. Remove from heat and cool about 15 minutes. Stir in pineapple chunks and lemon juice and pulp. Chill before serving by placing in a cooler or putting bottom of pan in cold water. Serve either plain or with whipped cream topping.

East Carson Bread Pudding

Serves 8
Preparation time: 1¼ hours

The east fork of the Carson River begins in the pine forest of the high Sierra and flows into the desert country of juniper and sagebrush. The vistas of snowcapped mountains are striking, and a natural hot springs pool at camp makes this a very relaxing trip.

Whole grain bread   4 cups (about 6 to 8 slices)
Medium apples   2
Medium lemon   1
Plain yogurt   ½ cup
Raisins   ⅓ cup
Cinnamon   to taste
Milk powder   ⅔ cup
Water   2 cups
Egg   1
Brown sugar   ¼ cup
Butter or margarine   1 tablespoon

Crumble bread into small pieces. Put ⅓ of the bread into the bottom of a well-seasoned 8-inch Dutch oven. Grate apples. Combine with lemon juice and pulp. Cover bread crumbs with ½ apples, yogurt, and raisins. Sprinkle cinnamon over top. Combine milk powder with water. Add egg and brown sugar to milk, stirring until smooth. Pour ½ this mixture over ingredients in Dutch oven. Place another ⅓ of the bread crumbs on top, then remaining apples, yogurt, raisins, and rest of bread crumbs. Pour milk mixture over top. Add cinnamon and top with pats of butter. Let pudding sit 20 to 30 minutes. Bake 45 minutes with 4 briquets underneath and 9 on top. Let cool slightly before serving.

Yogurt Dessert

Serves 6
Preparation time: 5 minutes

Plain yogurt   2 pounds
Honey   3 tablespoons
Vanilla   1 teaspoon
Cinnamon   to taste
Raspberries   15-ounce can

Combine yogurt with honey, vanilla, and cinnamon. Put in separate serving dishes and top with raspberries.

Androscoggin Dessert

Serves 8
Preparation time: 5 minutes

The Androscoggin River in New Hampshire has a steady year-round flow and the best white water in the state. In addition, this river has clean water, lovely spruce- and fir-lined banks, and good views of the Presidential Range. All these make it a popular run for canoeists and kayakers.

Applesauce   quart jar
Oatmeal cookies   16-ounce package

Open applesauce and cookies. All in the party serve themselves.

Index